D1608252

HOW BOSNIA ARMED

Marko Attila Hoare

HOW BOSNIA ARMED

Saqi Books
in association with
The Bosnian Institute

British Library Cataloguing-in-Publication Data
A catalogue for this book is available from the
British Library

ISBN 0 86356 367 8 (pb)
ISBN 0 86356 451 8 (hb)

EAN 9 780863 563676 (pb)
EAN 9 780863 564512 (hb)

copyright © 2004 Marko Attila Hoare

this edition first published 2004

Saqi Books
26 Westbourne Grove
London W2 5RH
www.saqibooks.com

in association with
The Bosnian Institute
14/16 St Mark's Road
London W11 1RQ
www.bosnia.org.uk

Acknowledgements

This book grew out of a research project that the author undertook in 1997–98 with the assistance of a grant from the Smith Richardson Foundation, awarded to him by International Security Studies of Yale University; he would therefore like to thank both these institutions for their support. The book itself was written while the author was in receipt of a Postdoctoral Fellowship from the British Academy, which he would like to thank for its past and continuing support. He would like to thank also the Press Centre of the Army of the Republic of Bosnia-Herzegovina for its donation to him of copies of many of the Bosnian Army publications cited in the text; and the Bosnian Institute for the use of its library and newspaper archive. Finally, special thanks go to Jovan Divjak, former Deputy Commander of the Bosnian Army, for agreeing to be interviewed by the author, for taking him on a tour of the Sarajevo battlefields and for lending him several of his own books; and to Nermin Mulalić, for his expert advice on the *mujahedin*. All views expressed by this text are, however, entirely those of the author.

Contents

Foreword

by

Brendan Simms

It has often been said that Bosnia was the most reported war in history. Yet it was only with the publication of Branka Magaš and Ivo Žanić's edited collection on *The War in Croatia and Bosnia-Herzegovina 1991–1995* two years ago that any systematic light was shed on the military and political course of the war itself. Now, with Marko Attila Hoare's *How Bosnia Armed* we finally have a detailed study of the origins and development of the Bosnian Army, the only legitimate and internationally recognized local force. This is the book I wished had been available when I was writing my study of British policy, *Unfinest Hour, Britain and the Destruction of Bosnia* (London 2001). Hoare's study, which is based on a very wide range of contemporary sources, is particularly useful for those like myself who do not read Bosnian (Croatian/Serbian). He shows that complex circumstances need not lead to the obfuscation and despair that characterized the dominant 'ancient hatreds' and 'all sides are equally guilty' schools of interpretation in 1992–5. For the author traces with consummate skill the emergence of the Bosnian Army from such disparate tributaries as the Muslim Patriotic League, the old communist Territorial Defence, the police of the Ministry of the Interior, deserters from the Yugoslav Peoples' Army (JNA), various criminal gangs, and even the Croat militias HVO and HOS.

Hoare both restores a sense of the complex context and the confusion of the early months, and at the same time makes clear the underlying pattern of events. For whereas the protagonists of 'Greater Serbia' had a very clear sense of their military and political objectives – the ethnic cleansing of Bosnia of non-Serb populations

– the Bosnian Muslims and those Serbs and Croats sympathetic to the idea of a multi-ethnic Bosnia had little idea of what was about to hit them. Only the most rudimentary military precautions were taken, and sometimes suspended in order not to 'provoke' the Serbs or the JNA; in a spirit of what retrospectively seems like suicidal conciliation, the Muslim leader Alija Izetbegović even allowed the disarming of the Bosnian territorial defence forces. Matters were complicated – and here the author's intimate knowledge of Bosnian high politics is deployed very effectively – by the persistence of strong Yugoslavist sentiments among Muslim elements within KOS, the ubiquitous federal intelligence services. All this helped to accentuate the decisive contribution of the much better prepared Bosnian Croat militia, the HVO, during the early stages of the war in central Bosnia, Mostar and western Herzegovina generally; the initially symbiotic relationship with the Bosnian state was reflected in the many Muslims which served in its ranks.

The Bosnian Army which emerged from the first shock of the Serb onslaught, as Hoare persuasively suggests, in many ways resembled the Communist-led Partisans of World War II. In each case, a broad-based resistance cohered around the primary victim of genocide: in 1941 Bosnian and Croatian Serbs, in 1992 Bosnian Muslims. The multi-ethnic character of the Bosnian army was thus both partly symbolic yet capable of development. That this development did not take place – that in fact there was a tendency towards ever greater ethnic exclusivity within the Armija – was as much as result of Western policy as the inevitable culmination of internal trends. The international community seemed determined to stifle Bosnia's fledging armed forces at birth: their prowess was systematically negated, particularly by the British, and contrasted with the warrior spirit and spit and polish of their separatist Serb adversaries; and an international arms embargo locked in place the technological inferiority with which the Bosnians had begun the war.

All this severely reduced the chances of a genuine multi-ethnic alternative developing through the Bosnian army. Even previously loyal Serbs and Croats lost any incentive to be slaughtered in a one-sided massacre. Separatist Croats were further emboldened to go their own way in central Bosnia and western Herzegovina; the precarious alliance with the HVO collapsed. Muslims serving in Croat formations were rounded up and suffered terribly. In response, as Hoare demonstrates, the Bosnian army radically improved its operational effectiveness, but also became ethnically increasingly homogeneous. Loyal Croats and Serbs continued to serve, particularly in urban areas such as Tuzla and Sarajevo, but in general terms the army evolved from a 'Bosnian' into a narrowly 'Bosniak' Muslim force. The resulting Byzantine sectarian squabbles are described in depressing and persuasive detail by the author.

What the Bosnian army never became was an 'Islamist' force. Hoare proves that it never embraced Bin Laden or any other form of Islamic fundamentalism. The foreign Muslim – principally Arab – volunteers proved to be locally unpopular and a political embarrassment; most of them were sent home after the Dayton Accords. Rather, though Hoare himself does not use the analogy, the Bosnian Army became 'Muslim-Nationalist' in a secular sense rather along the lines of Zionism. Despite successes against Croat separatists in central Bosnia, and impressive operations in Bihać and on the Kupres plateau, the Army struggled to carry the war to the aggressors. In part, this was due to the universal *campanilismo* which hobbled anything but local defence operations; and, of course, there was the arms embargo. But it also reflected the increasing failure of the Bosnian army to inspire the loyalty of moderate Serbs, Croats and Muslims, and the tendency of the Bosnian government to settle for a rump Muslim-dominated state. In this respect, as in some others, Hoare is right to conclude that the principal Muslim party, the SDA, became 'the accomplice of the project to partition Bosnia-Herzegovina along ethnic lines'. One might add that it had also become the accomplice of Western powers determined to force the Bosnians into an unjust settlement.

Centre of International Studies, University of Cambridge

Introduction

The Army of the Republic of Bosnia-Herzegovina (ARBiH) is one of the most enigmatic and controversial military phenomena to have appeared in recent history. Beginning life officially only in the spring of 1992 and in a position of apparent strategic hopelessness, it succeeded over the course of the next three-and-a-half years in fighting to a standstill the attempts of Bosnia-Herzegovina's larger and more powerful neighbours to destroy it. In the autumn of 1995 the ARBiH won a string of impressive victories that appeared to bring its Serbian enemy to the verge of total defeat, only for Bosnia-Herzegovina's political leadership to sign a cease-fire followed by a peace treaty that left the struggle unresolved. The Dayton Accord of November 1995 thus marked neither the ARBiH's victory nor its defeat. Equally uncertain was its political and ideological identity: either lauded as the defender of a multi-ethnic country or derided as the expression of an aggressive Muslim nationalism, the ARBiH's increasingly uni-national composition came to conflict increasingly with its official role as guardian of all Bosnia-Herzegovina's peoples. The ARBiH went from being a Bosnian Army at its birth in 1992 to a 'Bosniak army' by 1995 ('Bosniaks' being the official name for the Bosnian Muslims adopted by their leadership during the war).[1]

This is a brief history of the ARBiH that seeks to shed some light on these issues. It examines the dual origins of the ARBiH: on the one hand in the Territorial Defence (TO) force of Titoist Bosnia-Herzegovina, the locally based defence force organised by the

Communist authorities to resist a foreign invasion by a more powerful enemy; and on the other in the Patriotic League (PL), the clandestine resistance movement organised by the Muslim nationalists who won the first free elections in Bosnia-Herzegovina in the autumn of 1990 and thereafter increasingly controlled the Bosnian state. The birth and evolution of the ARBiH are traced under the impact of external and internal political events, as first Serbia and the Bosnian Serb nationalists then Croatia and the Bosnian Croat nationalists sought to tear Bosnia-Herzegovina apart. President of the Bosnian Presidency Alija Izetbegović and the Party of Democratic Action (SDA) were left in the paradoxical position of being a purely Muslim political force at the head of a multi-national Bosnian state, and of having to reconcile their integral Muslim nationalism with their formal commitment to the unity of this state, a unity that was impossible on the basis of domination by the Muslims or any single nationality. How they sought to resolve this contradiction largely determined the course of the ARBiH's history and the outcome of the Bosnian War.

The ARBiH was one of three armies to emerge from the Territorial Defence of Titoist Bosnia-Herzegovina. The others were the Army of the Serb Republic (VRS) and the Croat Defence Council (HVO). These three armies fought each other in the war of 1992–95, but they had a common institutional origin. The present work is primarily a history of the ARBiH and does not seek to examine the VRS or HVO in equal measure. Nevertheless, to situate the emergence of the ARBiH in its proper context it is necessary also to say a little about its rivals, born alongside it from the same womb. The VRS and HVO are therefore discussed in detail only insofar as they form part of the history of the ARBiH. Thus the formation of the VRS is traced up until the time it becomes an army wholly separate from the ARBiH. Likewise, the HVO is discussed as part of the 'Armed Forces of the Republic of Bosnia-Herzegovina', to which it formally belonged together with the ARBiH, as is the institutional relationship between the two armies that was never entirely broken off. The internal histories of the VRS and HVO are however beyond the scope of this work.

External perceptions of the Bosnian Army are complicated by accusations that Bosnia-Herzegovina's Muslim political and military leaders of the 1990s were 'Islamic fundamentalists', even that they had links to Osama bin Laden and al-Qaʿida. Since the terrorist attacks on New York and Washington of 11 September 2001 increased interest has been generated in the alleged 'Bosnia – bin Laden' connection, due in part to the presence of foreign '*mujahedin*' in Bosnia-Herzegovina during and after the war. This work therefore discusses the role of the *mujahedin* in the war and the truth about bin Laden's alleged involvement.

Acronyms

ARBiH	Army of the Republic of Bosnia-Herzegovina
HDZ	Croat Democratic Community
HOS	Croatian Armed Forces
HR H-B	Croat Republic of Herzeg-Bosna
HZ H-B	Croat Community of Herzeg-Bosna
HVO	Croat Defence Council
ICTY	International Criminal Tribunal for the Former Yugoslavia
IFOR	Implementation Force
JNA	Yugoslav People's Army
KOS	Counter-Intelligence Service
MUP	Ministry of Internal Affairs
OS RBiH	Armed Forces of the Republic of Bosnia-Herzegovina
PL	Patriotic League
RBiH	Republic of Bosnia-Herzegovina
RSK	Serb Republic of Krajina
SAO	Serb Autonomous Oblast
SDA	Party of Democratic Action
SDB	State Security Service
SDS	Serb Democratic Party
SFOR	Stabilisation Force
SFRJ	Socialist Federal Republic of Yugoslavia
SRBiH	Serb Republic of Bosnia-Herzegovina
SRJ	Federal Republic of Yugoslavia
SUBNOAR	Union of Associated Fighters of the People's Liberation Antifascist War
TO	Territorial Defence
VOPP	Vance-Owen Peace Plan
VRS	Army of the Serb Republic
VSRBiH	Army of the Serb Republic of Bosnia-Herzegovina

ONE

Origins of the Bosnian Army, 1941–1992

The Territorial Defence of the Socialist Republic of Bosnia-Herzegovina

The structural peculiarities of Bosnia-Herzegovina's armed forces date back to the years of the Partisan resistance movement led by the Communist Party of Yugoslavia in opposition to the Axis powers and their collaborators in occupied Yugoslavia. This struggle was waged under the banner of national self-determination for the constituent lands and peoples of Yugoslavia and the organisation and ideology of the 'People's Liberation Movement' reflected this. Thus, the Communists' Provincial Committee for Bosnia-Herzegovina was responsible for raising a guerrilla force on a specifically Bosnian basis: in 1941 this was referred to as 'The People's Liberation Army of Bosnia-Herzegovina' and was commanded by the 'General Staff of the People's Liberation Partisan Detachments of Bosnia-Herzegovina', with jurisdiction over all Bosnian territory. The Bosnian Partisans claimed that the 'People's Liberation Army of Bosnia-Herzegovina' was 'composed of Muslims, Croats and Serbs' and was fighting a 'decisive, ferocious struggle for the national liberation of Bosnia-Herzegovina'; they claimed that the 'great liberation army of Bosnians and Herzegovinians' was 'bringing liberation to all Muslims, all Croats and all Serbs.'[1] During and immediately after the war the Bosnian Communists founded the 'People's Republic of Bosnia-

Herzegovina' as a constituent 'state' of the Yugoslav federation, with its own specifically Bosnian presidency, government, parliament, constitution, flag and coat of arms. In 1948 a distinct 'Communist Party of Bosnia-Herzegovina' was officially proclaimed. This specifically Bosnian army-building, state-building and Party-building process nevertheless disguised an ethnic, political and social base that was highly diverse and differed greatly according to locality, something that was inevitable for a number of reasons: the fragmented character of Bosnia-Herzegovina's society; the small number of Communists at the war's start in 1941; their aim of building a broadly based resistance movement; and the decentralising conditions of guerrilla warfare. Each Party cell, each local council and each military unit had its own specific character; many recruited, or were infiltrated by, former members of anticommunist forces defeated by the Partisans – Serb Chetniks, Croat Domobrans, Muslim SS troops and others. For example, in Sarajevo the city bureaucracy was a well established professional body with a high proportion of Muslims and Croats that had served and survived earlier regimes: Austro-Hungarian, Yugoslav royal and Croatian quisling. Yet directly to the north in the mountainous rural regions of Ozren and Zvijezda the village councils and agrarian cooperatives were in the hands of Serb peasants whose sympathy often lay with a still-active Chetnik movement.[2]

Following the Communist seizure of power, control over Yugoslavia was rapidly concentrated in the hands of the Party and Federal centre: the self-government of Bosnia-Herzegovina and the other five constituent Yugoslav republics (Slovenia, Croatia, Serbia, Montenegro and Macedonia) remained purely formal, while the Partisan units were merged into a regular Yugoslav People's Army (JNA) with no space for unit autonomy. The lessons of World War II were not lost, however. The Soviet-Yugoslav split of 1948 led to the development during the 1950s of a 'Doctrine of General People's War' that aimed to mobilise the entire population for struggle in the event of a foreign invasion.[3] Following the Warsaw Pact invasion of Czechoslovakia in 1968, Yugoslavia's President Tito resolved to prepare for a similar attack on his country through a system of 'Territorial Defence' (TO) inspired by the Partisan method of warfare.[4] Territorially based units were removed from the command structure of the JNA and placed under the supervision of civilian authorities with staffs at the local, municipal and okrug level. Municipal councils had supervision over the weapons and munitions for their local forces and were obliged to provide facilities for their storage.[5] TO forces were also to be funded locally, something that strained municipal council budgets.[6] In 1974 the TO system was further devolved to the level of the 'socio-political commune' – as Tito said 'the centres of organised resistance must be every factory, every settlement, every portion of our territory. Territorial Defence units are prepared to carry out the struggle not only in conjunction with the Yugoslav Peoples Army but independently.'[7] Each Republic would have its own TO staff; in December 1969 Franjo Herljević became the first commander of the Republican Staff of the People's Defence of Bosnia-Herzegovina.

The dichotomy between Communist centralisation and Partisan decentralisation was thus resolved through the combination of a regular army at the Yugoslav Federal level with a localised system of territorial defence at the Republican level. JNA conscripts from Bosnia-Herzegovina might serve anywhere from Slovenia to Macedonia, but members of Bosnia-Herzegovina's TO served at their locality and place of work. Although the TO would provide the institutional structure through which the post-Communist Bosnian government could build a Bosnian Army in the 1990s, it was not one that could automatically encompass the entire Bosnian territory and population in the way the JNA once encompassed the whole of Yugoslavia. The subordination of the TO force of a given municipality, village or work-unit to the Republican Staff in Sarajevo was conditional on the loyalty of the relevant local political authority to the government in Sarajevo. Given that in the free elections of 1990 Bosnia-Herzegovina's population mostly voted along ethnic lines, with Muslims, Serbs and Croats each voting overwhelmingly for the principal Muslim, Serb and Croat 'national' parties respectively, this meant that in most Serb- or Croat-majority localities and some mixed ones the most influential political bodies became the local branches of the nationalist Serb Democratic Party (SDS) or Croat Democratic Union (HDZ). The relevant TOs consequently spawned units not of – or not only of – the ARBiH but also of its anti-Bosnian Serb- or Croat-nationalist counterparts – the VRS and HVO. As Hasan Efendić, the first commander of the ARBiH and a professional officer of the TO, says with regard to Herzegovina, 'The Territorial Defence in the municipalities with a Croat majority was transformed into the HVO while the Territorial Defence in Eastern Herzegovina was transformed into the Territorial Defence of the Serb Autonomous Oblast of Herzegovina. The remaining part of the TO went to the Bosniak nation.'[8]

Titoist policy had strengthened the authority of the Republics and Autonomous Provinces over military affairs. Each Republic and Autonomous Province possessed its own Territorial Defence force that was subordinate directly to the Supreme Command, which after Tito's death was the collective Presidency of the Socialist Federal Republic of Yugoslavia (SFRJ). The JNA General Staff was therefore bypassed. Furthermore, the JNA was organised in six armies that corresponded to the five larger Republics and the Autonomous Province of Vojvodina, as well as an independent corps that corresponded to the Socialist Republic of Montenegro. The JNA itself was therefore close to being federalised. In 1987 the JNA high command, under Defence Minister Branko Mamula and his deputy and successor Veljko Kadijević, rebelled against this military organisation and initiated a backlash aimed at restoring their authority in military affairs vis-a-vis the Republics. In Mamula's words, 'This meant excluding the Republican leaderships from the system of commanding the armed forces and armed struggle.'[9] The six armies were replaced by three army groups 'whose territorial division', in the words of Kadijević, 'completely disregarded the administrative borders of the Republics and Provinces.'[10] The staffs of the Republican and Provincial TOs were subordinated to the staffs of the three army groups, the staffs of the TO zones at the next level down to the staffs of the JNA corps. In Kadijević's words, 'It is certain that this solution, at least up to a point, removed the already developed control of the Republics and Provinces over their Territorial Defences and greatly reduced their already legalised influence over the JNA.'[11] The TO forces were also greatly reduced in size. The TO of the Socialist Republic of Bosnia-Herzegovina was therefore reduced from 293,272 soldiers at the start of 1987 to 86,362 by the end of 1991. Furthermore, this reduction was made disproportionately at the expense of Muslim- or Croat- rather than Serb-majority okrugs. Thus during 1988 the TO for the Muslim-majority Sarajevo okrug was reduced by 42.3%, but the TO for the Serb-majority Banja Luka okrug was reduced by only 16%.[12]

The TOs in Muslim-majority areas would nevertheless become the institutional basis for the defence of the Bosnian state. They could not assume this role, however, without a political leadership. The Bosnian Communist regime had made no preparations for the defence of Bosnia-Herzegovina from the approaching Serbian juggernaut prior to its fall in the autumn of 1990. Thus it was left to individual Bosnian officials and TO commanders to defend their respective spheres of the Bosnian state and armed forces from Serb-nationalist encroachment. On 14 May 1990, in response to the electoral victory of non-Communist parties in Slovenia and Croatia, the JNA General Staff ordered the confiscation of all TO armaments and their storage in JNA depots. This order was immediately passed on to the lower-level TO staffs by the Republican Staff of the TO for Bosnia-Herzegovina, headed by a Serb, Colonel-General Miloš Bajčetić. The order was eventually endorsed by the Communist-controlled Bosnian Presidency on 19 October. However, it ran into obstruction from some lower-level TO staffs, particularly those headed by Croats as well as that of the city of Sarajevo, which refused to hand over their armaments to the JNA. On 23 October the Republican Staff of the TO once again ordered the lower-level staffs to surrender their weapons. In the face of continued obstruction by the latter, the Republican Staff appealed to the Presidency to enforce the order. By this time, however, the Communist regime had fallen and the Bosnian state was in the hands of new political forces.

The November-December 1990 elections brought to power a coalition of three anticommunist nationally-based parties – the SDS, HDZ and SDA. The Bosnian state therefore fell into the collective hands of three parties with radically opposed political goals. The new Bosnian Presidency was composed of two Muslims (Alija Izetbegović and Fikret Abdić of the SDA), two Serbs (Nikola

Koljević and Biljana Plavšić of the SDS), two Croats (Stjepan Kljuić and Franjo Boras of the HDZ) and one 'Yugoslav' (Ejup Ganić of the SDA). The coalition of the three nationalist parties, upon taking power in the autumn of 1990, divided up the official and ministerial posts between themselves. Of the three posts with a direct bearing on Bosnian security, the SDA received the Interior Ministry; the HDZ received the Defence Ministry; and the SDS received the command of the Territorial Defence. These three institutions thereupon pursued mutually contradictory security policies. No genuine all-Bosnian security measures were possible on the basis of a coalition government of nationalist parties; with each coalition partner viewing at least one of the others as its principal enemy, any steps taken by one that affected the military position of the Republic were necessarily viewed as a threat by at least one of the others – it was a zero-sum game. The SDA, for its part, sought to cooperate with the JNA and other organs of the Bosnian and Yugoslav state that had remained in place following the change of regime. The Bosnian Presidency therefore endorsed the order for okrug-, city- and municipal-level staffs to surrender their weapons to the JNA. In this context, TO commanders such as Hasan Efendić, commander of the Sarajevo City TO, felt they had no option but to obey the order.[13]

So long as all three nationalist parties remained in the coalition, only the most token security measures could be taken at the official level. Thus on 7 February 1991 the Bosnian Presidency established a 'Council for All-People's Defence' and a 'Council for the Defence of the Constitutional Order', both recognised institutions of the Communist era. On 9 June the Presidency condemned the incursion into Bosnian territory of paramilitary forces of the 'Serb Autonomous Oblast of Krajina' in Serbian-occupied Croatia, but also called upon the JNA to safeguard Bosnia-Herzegovina's borders and territorial integrity. When on 21 September the Presidency voted to demand that the JNA withdraw Serbian and Montenegrin reservists from Bosnian territory, and to permit municipal councils to carry out a partial mobilisation of their Territorial Defence forces with its consent, Presidency member Plavšić voted against both measures. The Presidency also formed a 'Crisis Staff' comprised of

Presidency members Ganić, Plavšić, Boras; Interior Minister Alija Delimustafić; Defence Minister Jerko Doko and Bosnian Territorial Defence Commander Drago Vukosavljević. The Crisis Staff therefore represented a fair balance between the three Bosnian nationalities, but by the same token was powerless as an organ of state.[14] General Vukosavljević, TO Commander for Bosnia-Herzegovina from 1991, acted as an agent of the Serb-nationalist forces that were seeking to dismantle Bosnia-Herzegovina and establish a Great Serbian state. During the Croatian War of 1991 officers of Vukosavljević's Staff actively participated in the military operations against Croatia. At the end of 1991 Vukosavljević travelled to Belgrade and returned with an order compelling the Bosnian TO Staffs to surrender their heavy weapons not encompassed by the order of October 1990. This was endorsed by Izetbegović himself in an effort to appease the JNA, but once again ran into obstruction from the lower-level TO staffs. In the face of the Sarajevo City TO Staff's refusal to surrender its anti-aircraft cannon, Vukosavljević employed JNA special forces to seize the latter from its depots. The Bosnian TO staff was filled with SDS supporters and acquired a Serb majority among its officers and officials. Some subordinate staffs, such as the Okrug Staff for Banja Luka, acquired a wholly Serb membership. However, the presence of Muslims, Croats and pro-Bosnian Serbs in various key positions, such as Republican TO Chief of Staff Fikret Jakić, in turn hampered the efforts of Vukosavljević and his collaborators.[15]

The command structure of the TO of Bosnia-Herzegovina was therefore the scene of a power struggle that escalated during the autumn and winter of 1991–92 as the JNA waged war against Croatia and sought to mobilise Bosnian Serb manpower and Bosnian financial resources for this purpose, while simultaneously preparing for the next stage of the war: the assault on Bosnia-Herzegovina. The JNA sought to disarm the Bosnian TO units in Muslim- and Croat- majority areas and to keep them disarmed, while arming the TO units in Serb-majority areas and redistributing weaponry for use in the coming war. Vukosavljević and the Serb majority in the Republican Staff of the TO collaborated with this policy, while members of the non-Serb minority in the Republican

Staff and okrug and municipal staffs in Muslim- and Croat-majority areas sought to retain or regain control over their own armaments. Conversely, TO municipal-level staffs in Serb-majority municipalities conflicted with their senior, okrug-level staffs when the latter were dominated by Muslims or Croats. The key issue in the power struggle was control over the TO's weaponry that had been paid for by local and regional organs of government in Bosnia-Herzegovina but which the JNA had taken control of. Thus in October 1991 the Municipal Staffs of Žepče and Zavidovići in northern Bosnia, where Muslims and Croats outnumbered Serbs, sought the return of their weaponry from the JNA, while Muslim and Croat members of the Okrug Staff of Doboj sought personal weapons to defend themselves from the JNA. Conversely the Serb commander of the Municipal Staff for Bosanski Brod on his own initiative turned over TO military equipment to the JNA, while the TO commander for the predominantly Serb Glamoč municipality in south-west Bosnia, without informing the Okrug Staff at predominantly Croat Livno, took weapons from a JNA warehouse and distributed them to the local Serb population. In such a situation, with the formal chain of command increasingly disregarded in favour of covert collaboration among members of the same nationality, it was easy for individual commanders to come to grief. Jovan Divjak, commander of the Okrug Staff of Sarajevo, distributed weapons to the Municipal Staff in Croat-majority Kiseljak and was consequently relieved of his duty by the Serb-dominated Republican Staff.[16] Divjak subsequently became Deputy Commander of the ARBiH, the most senior ethnic-Serb officer to serve in it.

The Patriotic League

It was the SDA under whose umbrella active preparations for Bosnian military resistance were to be organised. The SDA stands in the long tradition of Muslim 'national' parties in Bosnia-Herzegovina that tried and succeeded in uniting the overwhelming majority of the Bosnian Muslim electorate behind their successive banners. Thus under Austria-Hungary the 'Muslim National

Organisation' exercised a dominant political influence among the Bosnian Muslims, as did the 'Yugoslav Muslim Organisation' under the interwar Yugoslav kingdom. As a vulnerable minority nationality under successive alien regimes, the Bosnian Muslims tended to close ranks and to give their support to a single political party at any given time; thus within the Muslim nation conditions were weighted against the development of political pluralism, with splinter parties that broke from the dominant Muslim party tending rapidly to fall into political oblivion. Muslim politics were however plagued by divisions between proponents of a 'Croat', 'Serb' or 'Yugoslav' orientation, and likewise between proponents of a 'religious' or a 'national' understanding of what it meant to be Muslim. So far as the SDA is concerned, its precursor was the 'Young Muslims', a radical organisation that appeared in 1939 as a defensive measure in the face of Serbian and Croatian efforts at partitioning Bosnia-Herzegovina. The Young Muslims rejected either a Croat or a Serb orientation in favour of an integral Muslim nationalism of an explicitly Islamic character. The Young Muslims grew in the years of the Ustasha regime of Bosnia-Herzegovina (1941–45) and in the early years of the Communist regime (1945–49), both of which appeared to threaten the survival of Bosnian Muslim society in its traditional form.[17] The Communists suppressed the Young Muslims; among those tried and imprisoned in the process was a youthful Alija Izetbegović. During the late 1960s, 1970s and early 1980s, however, as the Communist regime liberalised, the conditions were created for a new flowering of Muslim intellectual and cultural activity in Bosnia-Herzegovina. This in turn aroused fears among the Communist authorities of a 'Muslim nationalism' directed against them, fears heightened by the Islamic Revolution in Iran and the inspiration it undoubtedly provided to a section of educated Bosnian Muslim opinion. In 1983 the authorities arrested thirteen Muslims suspected of nationalist activities and links with Khomeini's Iran. One of the thirteen died in prison as a result of the beatings and mistreatment he received; the remaining twelve were sentenced to prison terms. Among them were the future leading lights of the SDA: Alija Izetbegović, Hasan Čengić, Omer Behmen, Džemaludin Latić and Edhem Bićakćić.[18] This experience of persecution may have hardened these individuals and inclined them to a conspiratorial political style, much as was the case with the Communists in the 1920s and 30s.

Izetbegović was arrested on the basis of a text, the *Islamic Declaration*, that he had written but not published in the late 1960s and that called for the formation of a unified Islamic republic for the Muslim peoples of the world: a 'great Islamic federation from Morocco to Indonesia and from tropical Africa to central Asia'.[19] This text was eventually published in Sarajevo in 1990 and subsequently became the basis for Serb- and Croat-nationalist accusations that Izetbegović was an Islamic fundamentalist. In fact, the *Islamic Declaration* was far from a call to the imposition of Islamic rule on the Bosnian Serbs and Croats; on the contrary, the text made no mention of Bosnia-Herzegovina and stated specifically that 'An Islamic order can be established only in countries in which Muslims comprise the majority of the population. Without this majority, the Islamic order is confined solely to the government (for the other element – Islamic society – is missing) and may transform itself into rule by force.'[20] Insofar as the *Islamic Declaration* had any influence on Izetbegović's politics in the 1990s, it may have inclined him to abandon support for a unified Bosnia-Herzegovina in which Muslims would be outnumbered by Christians in favour of a rump Bosnian republic with a Muslim majority, in which an Islamic society and therefore state would be possible. So far as relations with other religions and peoples were concerned, Izetbegović's brand of Islam was of the most moderate and tolerant variety. This was demonstrated in his subsequent work, *Islam between East and West*, in which he upheld Islam as falling between the extremes of Christian religiosity and Western secularism, as a system of values that merges the material and the spiritual in a golden medium.[21] The real significance of Izetbegović's religious devotion was that he equated the national and the religious, envisaging a homogenous national community for the Muslims that would be Islamic: neither secular nor fundamentalist, it would live in good-neighbourly relations with the Serbs and the Croats but would be distinct from them. Izetbegović was in practice a Muslim nationalist, not an Islamic fundamentalist; a moderate version of Islam was the system of morals by which he wished his nation to be governed.

As the Communist regime crumbled in the late 1980s, various non-Communist Muslim currents came to the surface and were drawn together by Izetbegović to form the SDA. Adil Zulfikarpašić, a Swiss-based multimillionaire exile from the Communist regime, claims that the original decision to found the SDA was made by him and Izetbegović in consultation with one another in Zürich on 24 February 1990.[22] Izetbegović himself, however, claims that he began working on the formation of the SDA already in November 1989. The party was originally conceived as an all-Yugoslav organisation and the fist steps in its formation were taken among the Muslim community in Zagreb.[23] According to the testimony of Maid Hadžiomeragić, one of the founding members of the SDA and a former family friend of Izetbegović, the latter organised the SDA on the basis of a clandestine network whose branches were permitted no knowledge of each other's activities. The founding meeting of the SDA was held in Sarajevo's Holiday Inn hotel on 27 March 1990, entirely on the basis of Izetbegović's personal decision and without any prior consultation with the other founding members. The new party's founding declaration stated that 'The Party of Democratic Action is a political Alliance of citizens of Yugoslavia who belong to the Muslim cultural-historical sphere, as well as other citizens of Yugoslavia who accept the programme and goals of the party.' It stated further that 'the Bosnian-Herzegovinian Muslims, both those who live in Bosnia-Herzegovina and those who live outside its borders, represent an autochthonous Bosnian nation, thus comprising one of the six historical nations of Yugoslavia, who have their own historical name, their ground under their feet, their history, their culture, their religion, their poets and writers; in a word, their past and their future.' The declaration called for 'the maintenance of Yugoslavia as a free union of peoples, in other words a federal state in its present federal borders' and emphasised 'our particular interest in the maintenance of Bosnia-Herzegovina as the common state of Muslims, Serbs and Croats.'[24] The declaration was signed by a 'Provisional Council' of forty prominent Muslims who neither at this time, nor at any other, ever actually assembled.

Izetbegović personally coordinated the various wings of this secretive party: the Executive Committee made up of the four founding members; the hard core of his supporters from among the victims of the 1983 show trial; the Zagreb wing of his supporters under Salem Šabić; the circle grouped around Zulfikarpašić; and eventually the supporters of Fikret Abdić based in Velika Kladuša in West Bosnia.

The SDA won an overwhelming majority of the Muslim vote in the November-December 1990 general election and gradually assumed a leading, ultimately dominant position in the Bosnian state. The SDA's political and organisational character had a number of consequences for the regime it established and therefore for the course of Bosnian history in the 1990s. As a loosely bound coalition, the SDA possessed no common party procedural rules, the effect of which was to concentrate all power in the hands of Izetbegović. Disgusted at the absolute power exercised by the latter within the SDA, Hadžiomeragić resigned his party post in May 1990 and soon after went on record as describing the SDA as 'the Party of Autocratic Action of Alija Izetbegović'.[25] Another early prominent SDA member who subsequently broke with the regime was Muhamed Borogovac of Tuzla, who writes that the SDA was built 'exclusively from the family connections of Izetbegović. Izetbegović in fact formed a private, not a Muslim state.'[26] Adil Zulfikarpašić and his close collaborator Muhamed Filipović broke with Izetbegović in September 1990, portraying the break as one between a liberal secular current represented by Zulfikarpašić and a conservative clerical wing represented by Izetbegović. However, the question of power and authority within the party may have been more important than ideology in producing the split between Izetbegović and Zulfikarpašić, with the latter claiming at the time that he and Filipović had been unwillingly forced out. Zulfikarpašić accused the SDA of adopting a 'classically Bolshevik method of organisation' and becoming a 'typical conspiratorial organisation on a totalitarian model'.[27]

Izetbegović's political method resulted in a very stable regime, but one that functioned without a proper legal framework. Ultimately all aspects of the Bosnian state and army would be subsumed within this 'informal' politics, with all key political decisions taking place behind the scenes, unaccountable to the courts, parliament or public. Of greater immediate consequence following its electoral victory in 1990, however, was the fact that the SDA's integral Muslim nationalism and anti-Communism had early on brought it into friendly contact with its fellow dissidents on the Serb side, in both Bosnia-Herzegovina and Serbia. Following the arrest and trial of Izetbegović and his associates in 1983, Serb dissident intellectuals had lobbied for their release. In 1985, Izetbegović's close associates Halid Čengić, Džemaludin Latić and Mustafa Spahić, as well as his daughter Lejla Akšamija and the wife of another Muslim political prisoner Azijada Kasumagić, met with a group of Serb dissidents in Belgrade, including Dobrica Ćosić, the father of late-twentieth-century Serb nationalism, in what one of the participants would later refer to as a 'Serb-Muslim Yalta'.[28] In this way an early alliance was formed between those who would later become the leading Serb and Muslim nationalists, an alliance which gave birth to the governing coalition that took power following the elections of November-December 1990. In January 1991 the newly elected Bosnian parliament appointed a coalition government formed from the three principal Muslim, Serb and Croat nationalist parties, the SDA, SDS and HDZ. The partition of Bosnia-Herzegovina between Serb, Muslim and Croat nationalists that was finally endorsed with the Dayton agreement of 1995 was in some sense the natural end-product of this alliance.

In response to signs of military preparation on the part of the Bosnian Serb nationalists, part of the SDA's membership was committed to the formation of a military organisation to safeguard Bosnian sovereignty and territorial integrity. Soon after the change of regime, on 19 December 1990 the SDA General Council convened an 'SDA Club' from among SDA delegates in the Bosnian parliament to assess conditions in all areas of Bosnian life, including defence. The Club assessed Bosnia-Herzegovina's defence requirements and capabilities and began to stockpile weaponry. From the Club would emerge the Patriotic League (PL).[29] In February 1991 the Executive Council of the SDA discussed the need for an organisation to defend Bosnia-Herzegovina and the Muslim nation, one that would be outside the control of the Interior Ministry. According to Hasan Čengić, he then suggested the formation of a military organisation to Deputy Prime Minister Rusmir Mahmutćehajić, and the two of them secured Izetbegović's agreement for the project in March. The PL was divided between a civilian wing under Izetbegović, Čengić and Mahmutćehajić and a military wing comprising Muslim officers who had defected from the JNA. The first all-Bosnian meeting of the military wing's representatives would take place in May at the foot of Mt Trebević, where it was decided to anchor it in the structure of the SDA.[30] It would provide an organisational umbrella to cells being formed for resistance by individuals at the local level. Thus in Sarajevo's Stari Grad municipality preparations for resistance were underway from early 1991 with the assistance of Stari Grad's Municipal Council President and Secretary for People's Defence, based upon the Civilian Defence units established by the Communist authorities. The following autumn the Old Town resistance was included within the jurisdiction of the PL Regional Staff.[31] Izetbegović presided over a gathering of 356 leading Muslim political, cultural and humanitarian figures from all over Yugoslavia at a meeting at the Office of the Police in Sarajevo on 10 June 1991 and spoke of the dangers facing the Muslim people as Yugoslavia collapsed.[32] The assembly issued a 'Proclamation' declaring that it was the 'wish of all Yugoslavia's Muslims' for a unified Bosnian citizens' republic with full equality for all nationalities.[33] At the same meeting, a 'Council of National Defence of the Muslim nation' was established as the military council of the SDA.[34] This was viewed by its founders as a response to the formation of a military council by the SDS.[35] At this time the military organisation received the name 'Patriotic League'.

These military preparations took place as the sky darkened over Bosnia-Herzegovina and the dangers of war became apparent to the more perceptive. Two Muslims were shot dead in the vicinity of Bratunac in East Bosnia in September 1991 and early the following month the Bosnian Croat village of Ravno in the Trebinje municipality was destroyed by the JNA. According to PL officer Rifat Bilajac, following the meeting of 10 June the General Staff of the PL prepared Sefer Halilović for his role as commander of the future Bosnian army. Izetbegović would accept Halilović's proposal for the organisation of Bosnia-Herzegovina's defences at a secret meeting on 2 December 1991 at the Sarajevo suburb of Hrasnica, where the PL General Staff was principally based.[36] Halilović's concept of a regular Bosnian army was given preference by Izetbegović, Čengić and Mahmutćehajić over proposals for a guerrilla army.[37] Another influence on the organisation and strategy of the PL was Croatia's General Martin Špegelj, one of the strongest Croatian supporters of a firm military alliance with Bosnia-Herzegovina and preemptive strikes against JNA garrisons, to whose assistance Halilović pays tribute.[38] On 7–8 February 1992 at the village of Mehurići near Travnik, at a secret meeting organised with the aid of the SDA's Travnik organisation, the leaders of the PL formulated the tasks of their military organisation so as to coordinate its cells throughout the country.[39] On 25 February the General Staff of the PL at Hrasnica drew up a 'Directive for the defence of the sovereignty of Bosnia-Herzegovina', that defined the PL's task as 'the defence of the Muslim nation and the safeguarding of the integrity and unity of Bosnia-Herzegovina, so as to safeguard the further coexistence of all the nations and nationalities on the state territory of Bosnia-Herzegovina' and envisioned a military liberation of the country within sixty-seven days.[40] It aimed at the defence of the Podrinje region in East Bosnia through the disarming of JNA garrisons and the destruction of the bridges on the Drina river linking Bosnia-Herzegovina to Serbia.[41]

Serbia Prepares to Attack

Serbia's preparations for war against her neighbour were laid with tremendous determination, despite the fatal contradictions in their conception. The Army of the Serb Republic (VRS) was initially named the Army of the Serb Republic of Bosnia-Herzegovina (VSRBiH). Unlike the ARBiH, it was formed by an external, non-Bosnian party: namely, the Milosević regime in Belgrade in conjunction with the command of the JNA. According to Yugoslav Secretary for People's Defence Veljko Kadijević, the most senior figure in the JNA, from mid-1991 the JNA saw its tasks as: '1) The defence of the Serb nation in Croatia and its national interests; 2) the withdrawal of the JNA garrisons from Croatia; 3) full control of Bosnia-Herzegovina with the ultimate goal of defending the Serb nation and its national rights when that becomes actual; and 4) the establishment and defence of a new Yugoslav state of those Yugoslav nations who want it, in this phase the Serb and Montenegrin nations. Such changed tasks were accommodated and were the basic idea behind the use of armed forces.'[42] The VRS was formed by the JNA, acting under orders from Milošević, as part of this strategy. The JNA had begun to arm the SDS militia already in the spring of 1991.[43] However it was the JNA and the TO in Serb-majority areas of Bosnia-Herzegovina that were to form the basis of the new Bosnian Serb army, with the SDS militia of only secondary importance. A central role in the construction of the VSRBiH was played by the 9th Corps of the JNA, based in the Croatian town of Knin. Knin was at the heart of the Serb rebellion in Croatia that began in mid-1990, and it was there that the first showdown between Croatian forces and the JNA took place with the so-called 'Log Revolution' of August of that year. Although the Knin Corps was based outside Bosnia-Herzegovina it nevertheless provided the embryonic VSRBiH with key logistical, military and organisational support.

Ratko Mladić, the future Commander of the VSRBiH, served as Chief of the Department for Instruction of the 3rd Military District based in Skopje in 1989–91, and as assistant to the Commander of the Priština Corps in Kosovo from 14 January 1991 until the eve of the war in Croatia. On 26 June 1991 he was informed by Colonel-General Zivota Avramović, Commander of the 3rd Military District, that he was being transferred to Knin 'by the decision of the Supreme Command'. Following his arrival in Knin, Mladić served as Chief of the Department for Operational-Instructional Affairs until 31 July. As Mladić notes, 'our corps was one of the smallest in the JNA at that time' and had three garrisons, in Knin, Benkovac and Sinj. It was for part or all of 1991 under the direct command of the JNA General Staff.[44] At the end of July Mladić visited the JNA General Staff to receive direct instructions on military action to be taken in Croatia.[45] Mladić's relocation to Knin appears to have been part of the JNA's reorganisation in preparation for the wars in Slovenia and Croatia. His former superior, General Avramović, was appointed Commander of the 5th Military District, covering Slovenia and Croatia, at the start of July 1991. Avramović, a Serb, replaced the former 5th Military District Commander General Konrad Kolšek, a Slovene, who was transferred to Belgrade. At this time the officer corps of the 5th Military District was officially reported to be 57% Serb.[46] The Croatian government denounced the appointment of Avramović as 'unlawful', noting that none of the brigade and corps commanders, nor the four key officers in command of the 5th Military District, were Croats.[47]

The Commander of the Knin Corps at the time of Mladić's arrival there was Spiro Niković, a Serb, while the Chief of Staff was Janež Rebo, a Slovene. Most Croat officers rapidly left the Corps in the weeks that followed, so that the JNA in Knin became increasingly a purely Serb army. Mladić replaced Rebo as Chief of Staff, it appears, on 31 July, so that from then on the two highest functions in the Corps were both held by Serbs. According to Mladić, 'of great significance was the cooperation with the organs of government in the zone of responsibility of the Corps' – i.e. the organs of the Serb Republic of Krajina (RSK). Mladić claims that he recruited the local Serb population of the region into the ranks of the Corps to compensate for the shortage of manpower that the departure (or expulsion) of the Croat cadres had accentuated.[48] Mladić achieved a solid cooperation with the RSK forces, cemented on 26 August when his units and the RSK police under Milan Martić destroyed the Croat village of Kijevo.[49] Martić as RSK Minister of Internal Affairs formed Territorial Defence forces, from among the local Serb population, that served under the JNA.[50] On 10 March 1992, shortly before his departure from Knin, Mladić described the JNA and Territorial Defence of the RSK as forming a 'united organism' in which no division existed.[51] The SFRJ Presidency members for Serbia, Montenegro, Kosovo and Vojvodina staged a *coup d'état* in the SFRJ Presidency on 3 October 1991. SFRJ Vice-President of the Presidency Branko Kostić declared that he would assume the role of President in the absence of Croatia's Stipe Mesić who was President of the Presidency. This so-called 'rump Presidency' then assumed the right as Supreme Commander to give orders to the JNA, a role that rightfully belonged to the eight-member Presidency as a whole. The day following this *coup*, on 8 October the rump Presidency by its decree no. 1/49 promoted Colonel Mladić to the rank of Major-General while another Knin Corps officer, Zdravko Tolimir, was promoted to Lieutenant-Colonel.[52] Serbian President Slobodan Milošević, Croatian President Franjo Tuđman and UN representative Cyrus Vance signed the so-called Geneva Accord for a cease-fire in Croatia on 23 November 1991. According to the terms of this Accord the JNA was to begin withdrawing its forces from Croatia.[53] Following the signing of the Geneva Accord the Serbian leadership set about the creation of a Bosnian Serb army with the intention of transferring the war to Bosnia-Herzegovina. As Borisav Jović mentions in his diary on 5 December, Milošević aimed 'to withdraw all citizens of Serbia and Montenegro from the JNA in Bosnia-Herzegovina in a timely fashion and transfer citizens of Bosnia-Herzegovina to the JNA there', prior to the international recognition of Bosnia-Herzegovina, in order to 'create the possibility for the Serb leadership in Bosnia-Herzegovina to assume command over the Serb part of the JNA, just as the Muslims and Croats have already done.'[54] SFRJ Secretary for People's Defence Veljko Kadijević, the top figure in the JNA, according to Jović did not initially favour this proposal but agreed to consider it nonetheless.

While the Milošević regime and the JNA General Staff worked from above to organise a Bosnian Serb army, the SDS and its sympathisers in the officer corps of the JNA and TO were preparing for the coming war at the grass-roots level. The process of establishing a separate Bosnian Serb 'state' began in 1991, before the war in Croatia, at a time when the Bosnian Muslim leadership was still committed to the territorial integrity of Yugoslavia. Following the free elections of late 1990 the municipalities that fell under the control of the SDS began forming regional associations of 'Serb municipalities' as expressions of Serb self-rule at the local level. In September 1991 these regional associations grew into autonomous regional bodies. Thus the 'Serb Autonomous Oblast' (SAO) of

Herzegovina was established on 12 September, followed by the Autonomous Region of Bosanska Krajina on the 17th and the SAO of Romanija on the 19th. The SAOs of Semberija and North Bosnia were subsequently established, bringing the total to five. These SAOs were autonomous regional bodies that grouped together Serb-controlled municipalities, violating the authority of the central government in Sarajevo. When the Bosnian parliament prepared to vote in favour of the sovereignty of the Socialist Republic of Bosnia-Herzegovina on 24 October, the SDS delegates seceded from the parliament in protest and established a separate 'Serb National Assembly' claiming to represent the Bosnian Serb population as a whole. On 9–10 November the SDS held a referendum, restricted to the Bosnian Serb population in the areas under its control, allegedly to determine whether the Bosnian Serbs wished to live in an independent Bosnia-Herzegovina or to remain within Yugoslavia; the SDS leadership claimed a large majority voted for the latter option. On 11 December the Bosnian Serb assembly called upon the JNA to protect 'as integral parts of the state of Yugoslavia' the territories in Bosnia-Herzegovina in which the referendum had been held. Bosnian Serb military preparations for war ran in tandem with the political. By October 1991, the first artillery pieces were in place on Mt Trebević overlooking Sarajevo. In November 1991 the SDS took military control of the ski resort of Pale outside Sarajevo, a centre of JNA operations and a municipality where Radovan Karadžić possessed both personal influence and private property. The leadership of the Pale SDS at this time sacked the Muslim commanding officers of the Pale TO and replaced them with Serb officers.[55] On 11 November 1991 Bosnian TO Commander Vukosavljević ordered the transfer of an anti-aircraft battery with 4,000 shells from the 'Zrak' warehouse in Sarajevo to the outskirts of the city, from where the following spring they would be used to bombard the Bosnian capital.[56]

The JNA's 'withdrawal' from Croatia according to the terms of the Geneva Accord provided it with a cover for the redeployment of its forces in Bosnia-Herzegovina. Thus on 10–12 December it was reported that a convoy from the evacuated Plešo barracks outside Zagreb had arrived in Banja Luka and that a convoy of 38 military vehicles had left the Marshal Tito Barracks in Zagreb and headed for Bosnia-Herzegovina.[57] The Milošević regime was able to create a Bosnian Serb army under the nose of the UN. Jović wrote on 25 December that 'Veljko reports that 90% of the military has been dislocated in accordance with our talk on 5 December. Right now, 10–15% of the forces in Bosnia-Herzegovina are not from that republic.'[58] This decision was taken following extensive negotiations between Belgrade and the Bosnian Serb leaders, who appear to have favoured the formal withdrawal of the JNA from Bosnia-Herzegovina so that Bosnian Serb conscripts could be released from military service in other parts of the former Yugoslavia and return home for deployment against the Muslims and Croats. According to the so-called 'RAM' plan, the JNA following its redeployment was to arm Bosnian Serb paramilitary forces organised by the SDS, forming a new 'Bosnian Serb' army. Leading officers of the Knin Corps, as the formation that spear-headed the JNA campaign in Croatia, were during this period transferred to high positions in Bosnia-Herzegovina. On 28 November 1991 both Spiro Niković and Vladimir Vuković, who replaced him as Knin Corps commander in mid-September, were promoted to the rank of Major-General by the rump Presidency.[59] The Command of the 5th Military District reported on 30 December 1991 that all its forces had been withdrawn from Slovenia and Croatia and redistributed to the territories of the Republics of Bosnia-Herzegovina, Serbia and Montenegro.[60] On the same day the rump Presidency issued an order on the reorganisation of the JNA, establishing four military districts. The 2nd Military District was seated in Sarajevo and had jurisdiction over the Knin Corps, which remained on Croatian territory. At this point Milutin Kukanjac was appointed Commander of the 2nd Military District, Niković was appointed Commander of the 10th Corps based in Bihać, Vuković was appointed Commander of the 5th Corps based in Banja Luka and Mladić was promoted to Commander of the Knin Corps. Mladić was therefore directly subordinate to Kukanjac, based in Sarajevo.[61]

The military reorganisation of 30 December appears to have been made in preparation for the JNA's assault on Bosnia-Herzegovina. West Bosnia was now covered by the 5th, 9th and

10th Corps, each of which was commanded by a Serb general who had served or was serving as Commander of the Knin Corps. Of the Knin Corps' five brigades one, the 11th Motorised Brigade, was based in Bosnia-Herzegovina in the town of Bosansko Grahovo. Also on 30 December 1991 the JNA General Staff ordered the arming of the Bosnian Serb TO units – these had begun to be formed during the second half of 1991 in the territory controlled by the SAOs.[62] This arming of the Serb population of Bosnia-Herzegovina would be carried out using weapons and munitions earlier confiscated from the Bosnian TO or distributed from the JNA's own arsenals.[63] Thus at Pale a Serb Military Command was established within the framework of the Territorial Defence, which united the municipal government, Station of Public Security, Secretariat for People's Defence and other local organs of government behind a single military organisation. JNA equipment withdrawn from Mostar, Kiseljak, Visoko and other places was relocated to Pale and placed in the hands of the Military Command. JNA artillery regiments withdrawn from the predominantly Muslim or Croat towns of Visoko and Kiseljak were deployed around Sarajevo to enforce the siege.[64]

The Army of the Serb Republic

The 'Serb Republic of Bosnia-Herzegovina' (SRBiH), often referred to subsequently by its Serbian name of 'Republika Srpska', was formally established on 9 January 1992. By the time of the Bosnian declaration of independence in March 1992, one-third of Bosnia-Herzegovina's territory was in the hands of the SDS's five SAOs, while present on Bosnian territory were the Sarajevo, Tuzla, Banja Luka, Bihać, Bileća, Maribor and parts of the Knin, Zagreb, Rijeka, Podgorica, and Užice Corps of the JNA, altogether approximately 100,000 troops.[65] The rump Yugoslav Presidency held an expanded session on 2 February 1992 at which the political leaders of Serbia, Montenegro, the RSK and the Bosnian Serbs were present, as well as senior JNA officers including Chief of Staff Blagoje Adžić, Colonel-General Kukanjac and Major-General Mladić. This meeting, attended by a total of 37 participants, was called to put pressure on

RSK President Milan Babić to accept the Vance Plan that would bring UN peace-keepers into the Serb-held territories in Croatia.[66] This plan essentially allowed the JNA to end its losing war in Croatia and to withdraw its forces to Bosnia-Herzegovina, while the UN peacekeepers would guard the RSK from a possible Croatian counter-offensive. Jović consequently deemed the Vance Plan to be 'exceptionally favourable to the Serbian side'.[67] Mladić, Vuković and Niković met with Adžić in Bihać on 10 February and briefed him on the situation in their fields of responsibility. On this occasion Adžić stated publicly that 'if attempts are made to outmanoeuvre the peace operation by force or in any other way, the Army will be ready to protect the Serb people at any cost'.[68] At the same time Vuković requested that Mladić assist him in operations against Croat forces in south-west Bosnia. As a result of this agreement, units of the Knin Corps were deployed in the Kupres valley.[69] The Knin Corps captured Kupres from its Croat defenders on 8 April. At this time the Corps Command was still based in. Knin, overseeing the 'withdrawal' of its forces from Croatia into Bosnia-Herzegovina. Following the operation at Kupres Mladić returned to the Knin region to oversee further operations against the Croatian Army in Lika and northern Dalmatia.[70] Mladić by his own account left part of the Knin Corps' equipment employed during the Kupres operation in southern Bosnia, where he and his collaborators organised the 2nd Krajina Corps from the existing 10th (Bihać) Corps. Consequently on the eve of full-scale war in Bosnia-Herzegovina the JNA possessed two large and well-equipped corps in West Bosnia: the 1st Krajina Corps – formerly the 5th (Banja Luka) Corps – and the 2nd Krajina Corps. In Mladić's words, 'Those two corps were the basis for the formation of the Army of the Serb Republic.'[71]

The SRBiH declared independence on 27 March 1992. On 3 April the JNA bombarded Mostar and the following day Serb paramilitary forces occupied Banja Luka, the second city of Bosnia-Herzegovina. The JNA would expel Bosnian forces from the left bank of the river Neretva in Mostar only after fierce fighting, but Banja Luka – where the SDS had already established control of the town and municipal councils and which was the largest JNA military centre in the country – fell without a struggle.[72] The 'Federal Republic of Yugoslavia' (SRJ) was formally proclaimed on 27 April 1992 and consisted of the Republics of Serbia and Montenegro. Since all of Bosnia-Herzegovina lay outside the SRJ, the Serbian leadership was now compelled to divide the JNA into formally separate SRJ and Bosnian Serb armies. Milošević, Kostić, Jović, Montenegrin President Momir Bulatović and acting JNA Chief of Staff Života Panić met with the Bosnian Serb leaders Radovan Karadžić, Momčilo Krajišnik and Nikola Koljević on 30 April to arrange the formation of the Bosnian Serb army. As Jović wrote, 'we discussed the need to withdraw the remainder of the soldiers who are SRJ citizens from Bosnia-Herzegovina. Even without them, there remain around 90,000 JNA soldiers in that republic, mostly of Serb nationality, over whom the Serb leadership from Bosnia-Herzegovina can assume political command.' Furthermore, the participants arranged the formation of a command for the projected Bosnian Serb army. According to Jović, 'Since it is also necessary to withdraw generals who are not originally from Bosnia-Herzegovina, it was agreed that Gen. Mladić would replace Gen. Vuković. For us, this action was very significant, but for the Serbs in Bosnia-Herzegovina, I believe, it was even more significant. They got their own military.' One week later Jović notified Marrack Goulding, UN undersecretary for peacekeeping operations, that 'if there is no agreement among the three nations [of Bosnia-Herzegovina] it is not out of the question that command over the Serb part of the army will be assumed by the leadership of the Serb Republic of Bosnia-Herzegovina.'[73]

The decision to appoint Mladić Bosnian Serb military commander was therefore made by the political leaderships of Serbia and Montenegro and by the JNA in consultation with the Bosnian Serb leadership. Consequently in early May 1992 Colonel-General Blagoje Adžić, JNA Chief of Staff and acting SFRJ Secretary for People's Defence, summoned Mladić to Belgrade where they held an extensive discussion over military strategy. Upon returning to Knin, Mladić immediately received a message from Adžić ordering him to surrender his functions and travel once again to Belgrade where he would receive a new position from his superior, Colonel-

General Milutin Kukanjac. Upon arriving in Belgrade for the second time, Mladić was told by Adžić that he (Mladić) would assume the role of both Commander and Chief of Staff of the 2nd Military District in Sarajevo. Mladić thereupon travelled to Sarajevo to establish his new staff.[74] At about the same time Branko Kostić, as acting President of the rump Presidency and consequently head of the self-proclaimed Supreme Command of the Yugoslav armed forces, ordered Kukanjac to surrender his duties to Mladić and to travel to Belgrade. On 8 May 1992 the rump Presidency dismissed Kukanjac from active service and accepted the resignation of Adžić, who insisted on leaving out of solidarity with Kukanjac.[75] Belgrade TV reported on the afternoon of 9 May that Mladić had replaced Kukanjac that morning as Commander of the 2nd Military District, but added significantly that 'he will be there briefly because a higher post is awaiting him.' Meanwhile the same report indicated that Mladić's departure from the Knin Corps did not imply that the latter was ceasing to function, for the new Knin Corps commander General Savo Kovačević, who had served as Chief of Staff under Mladić, was reported as being engaged in the mobilisation of fresh Territorial Defence forces from the population of the territory of the RSK, including from those who had up till then served outside the Knin region. Kovačević indicated that a parallel programme of local mobilisation was being carried out in the neighbouring region of Bosanska Krajina (West Bosnia).[76]

Mladić relates that 'When I took up duty in the 2nd Military District I immediately assigned myself the task of assembling men and forming a command and General Staff, partly from the remnants of the 2nd Military District and partly from the men who had come with me from Knin and from other areas, who were born in Bosnia-Herzegovina… We immediately began the formation of a General Staff of the Serb Army.'[77] On 12 May the self-declared 'Assembly of the Serb Nation of Bosnia-Herzegovina' in Banja Luka resolved to establish formally the Army of the Serb Republic of Bosnia-Herzegovina. The Assembly voted to appoint Lieutenant-Colonel-General Ratko Mladić as Commander of the Supreme Staff and to take control of all JNA units on the territory of the SRBiH. Units of the VSRBiH thus established were to wear the same uniforms and epaulettes as the former JNA and Territorial Defence.[78] Mladić travelled at this time to Banja Luka to receive this appointment from SRBiH President Karadžić and the SRBiH Assembly delegates.[79]

Although the Assembly of the SRBiH passed a law establishing the VSRBiH on 12 May, the SRBiH Presidency did not promulgate this law until 19 May.[80] On this date the SDS militia and Serb Territorial Defence were unified to form the VSRBiH. 19 May was, not coincidentally, the date of the JNA's formal withdrawal from Bosnia-Herzegovina. Prior to that date Bosnian Serb military forces had been termed the 'Serb Territorial Defence' and as such were considered to be subordinate to the JNA, just as the Territorial Defence throughout the former Yugoslavia had been subordinate to the JNA. The nomenclature suggests that the Bosnian Serb armed forces considered themselves in some sense part of the Yugoslav armed forces until 19 May, i.e. until those armed forces had left the territory of the SRBiH and a separate Bosnian Serb army became necessary, for the 'Law on People's Defence' of 28 February 1992 which regulated the SRBiH's defence system, including the Territorial Defence, was considered to fall within the framework of the SFRJ law on defence.[81] Illustrative of the extent of the coordination between the withdrawal of the JNA and the establishment of the VSRBiH is the fact that the 'Presidency of the Serb Autonomous Region of Semberija and Majevica', as a body subordinate to the Presidency of the SRBiH, resolved on 9 May to transform all JNA units on its territory into the 'Serb Territorial Defence' and that the transformation would be completed by 19 May. In this way, by the time the JNA had 'withdrawn' from Bosnia-Herzegovina all its units remaining in the Semberija-Majevica region would be incorporated into the Bosnian Serb military framework.[82] The JNA's official 'withdrawal' from Bosnia-Herzegovina in May 1992 involved only the 14,000 troops who were citizens of the new Yugoslav state proclaimed on 27 April (i.e. native to Serbia or Montenegro); the remaining 80,000 were transferred to the TO forces of the Serb Republic. When the JNA finally withdrew from Sarajevo's Marshal Tito Barracks on 6 June 1992, it merely redeployed a couple of miles south to the Serb-held suburb of Lukavica.

The mainstay of the new army was, according to Mladić, the 1st and 2nd Krajina Corps which he himself had helped to organise, while the former JNA forces in East Bosnia – the 4th (Sarajevo) and 17th (Tuzla) Corps – were of much lower military value.[83] These corps were nevertheless converted into the Sarajevo-Romanija and North-East Bosnia Corps of the VSRBiH respectively. A fifth corps, the former 13th (Rijeka) Corps of the JNA withdrawn from Croatia, became the VSRBiH's Herzegovina Corps. Colonel Zdravko Tolimir, Chief of the Security Administration (better known as KOS) for the Knin Corps under Mladić and one of his closest advisors, entered the General Staff of the VSRBiH as Assistant Commander for Intelligence and Security and subsequently became Deputy Chief of Staff. In September 1992 the Karadžić regime took the final set of measures aimed at establishing a unified and 'independent' Bosnian Serb 'state'. The 'Serb Republic of Bosnia-Herzegovina' finally dropped the Bosnian appellation and became simply the 'Serb Republic'. The VSRBiH thereupon became the VRS. Whereas the ARBiH was formed by the Bosnian political leadership on the basis of the existing Republican institutions of Bosnia-Herzegovina, the formation of the VRS was the work of the Milošević regime in Belgrade and the JNA General Staff, with the SDS playing only a secondary role. The kernel of the VRS general staff came from the JNA's Knin Corps, a non-Bosnian military unit. The war in Bosnia-Herzegovina between the ARBiH and the VRS was therefore not simply a civil war between forces controlled by the Bosnian leadership and those controlled by the SDS. It began as a war between the native armed forces of Bosnia-Herzegovina and the proxy forces of the neighbouring state of Serbia – both Bosnian and non-Bosnian. As the war progressed, however, and the Milošević regime gradually lost control over its Bosnian Serb proxies, while the Bosnian state itself unravelled, the war increasingly lost the character of an inter-state conflict and assumed the character of a civil war between the Bosnian government forces and Bosnian Serb nationalists.

On the Eve of Total War

The military preparations of the PL in the period up to April 1992 were the clandestine efforts of an underground body to establish an organisational framework for future resistance. The PL was linked to one of the parties of government; its existence and activities were in no sense government policy, nor was a government defence policy possible. Of the three coalition partners in government from January 1991, the SDS was implacably opposed to any military preparations at the republican level or any arming of Croats and Muslims; HDZ leaders were interested only in the formation of autonomous Croat militias at the local level; while the SDA ministers and Presidency members continued to put their faith in a peaceful and negotiated solution to Bosnia-Herzegovina's rapidly escalating crisis. Most SDA politicians neither believed war would break out, nor prepared their constituents in any way for its possibility, but guided Bosnia-Herzegovina toward independence in the naive belief that this could be achieved without war. The Bosnian parliament voted in favour of a referendum on independence on 25 January 1992; this was held on 29 February – 1 March. On 2 March, after the announcement of a referendum victory for Bosnian independence was followed by the setting up in Sarajevo of barricades and counter-barricades by Serb nationalists and Bosnian patriots respectively, Izetbegović agreed to the formation of joint patrols by the JNA and police to negotiate the dismantling of the barricades.[84] Following the declaration of Bosnian independence on 3 March, Izetbegović continued naively to believe that the JNA on Bosnian soil could be worked with to prevent inter-communal fighting and could eventually be transformed into a Bosnian army. His own preparations for the defence of the state were therefore vacillating and half-hearted. Halilović was unable to obtain the President's authorisation for the PL's Directive for the Defence of the Sovereignty of Bosnia-Herzegovina and was accused by SDA vice-president Omer Behmen of being a warmonger.[85] Izetbegović subsequently confessed that after forty years' talk of 'brotherhood and unity' he did not expect the JNA to carry out genocide against Muslims.[86] On 11 March 1992 the Bosnian Presidency finally rescinded the order to the TO to surrender its weapons to the JNA. However, the Presidency neglected to inform the TO staffs of the change, weakening the TO officers in their confrontation with the JNA over the question of the confiscated weapons.[87] When on 1 April 1992 paramilitary forces from Serbia proper known as the 'Tigers' invaded the strategically key town of Bijeljina in the northeastern corner of Bosnia-Herzegovina to begin a reign of terror against its non-Serb inhabitants, Izetbegović sanctioned the JNA's occupation of the town two days later.[88] While it is true that the SDA laid the organisational foundations for a Bosnian resistance, the party's leaders did not prepare the Bosnian population politically or psychologically for war; such a preparation was made impossible by their governmental alliance with the Serb nationalists, their desire to conciliate the JNA and above all the inability of the SDA, as a wholly Muslim party, to appeal in any way to over fifty percent of Bosnia-Herzegovina's population. The success or failure of resistance to Serbian aggression would depend wholly on the competence of the PL, SDA or other bodies at the local level. Where they failed to offer any resistance, as in Foča or Višegrad, the Serbian conquest proceeded smoothly.

Izetbegović was, indeed, at the head of a state that had only just ceased to view him officially as its enemy. Izetbegović and other SDA ministers, such as Hasan Čengić and Omer Behmen, had been tried and imprisoned by the Communist authorities as 'Islamic fundamentalists' in 1983, Izetbegović being released only in 1988. The Muslim anti-Communists' assumption of power in December 1990 did not mean that their adherents would immediately cease to be persecuted by the state security services that had persecuted them during the decades of Communist rule. The period from December 1990 until the outbreak of full-scale war in the spring of 1992 witnessed the paradox of the Bosnian state continuing to clash with the army being organised to defend it by its own leading party of government. Bosnia-Herzegovina's Ministry of Internal Affairs (MUP) was by all accounts riddled with hostile agents, not only Serb and Croat nationalists but conservatives loyal to Belgrade of all nationalities. The setting up of barricades in Sarajevo by Serb nationalists on 2 March 1992 was assisted by SDS members of the

Sarajevo police.[89] Bosnian TO Commander General Vukosavljević, for his part, endorsed the 'referendum' organised by the SDS to legitimise the establishment of an independent 'Serb Republic' and ordered members of his Staff to vote in favour.[90]

The Muslim Alija Delimustafić, Minister of Internal Affairs until May 1992 and a protégé of the traitorous Presidency member Fikret Abdić, was a collaborator of the JNA's Counter-Intelligence Service (KOS – military intelligence) and the Federal police in the struggle with the PL and organised joint patrols by the police and JNA to combat the latter.[91] According to the testimony of KOS Chief Aleksandar Vasiljević himself, Delimustafić had employed the Bosnian police to defend the JNA's movements and supply lines while suppressing movements of arms and troops by Croat paramilitary forces; without this help the JNA could not have waged war in Croatia.[92] According to another Serbian source, the journalist of the Yugoslav secret services Marko Lopušina, it was thanks to Delimustafić's collaboration that Serbia and the JNA were able to wage war in Croatia in 1991 without a second front being opened in Bosnia-Herzegovina.[93] Delimustafić also agreed with Vasiljević to permit the JNA to 'defend' Bosnia-Herzegovina's TV relay stations, and clashed with the chief of the Bosnian State Security Service (SDB) Munir Alibabić-Munja when the latter arranged for Special Forces to defend the radio-television station in Sarajevo.[94] Delimustafić responded in December 1991 to accusations that he was a KOS agent by arguing that 'I have already several times publicly explained my negotiations with members of the security organs of the JNA. The fact is that we are by the nature of our work forced to collaborate. In short, the results of these negotiations – a peaceful Bosnia-Herzegovina – are much more important than the ridiculous accusation that I am a KOS agent.' He described his success in disarming Bosnian paramilitary forces as 'the fruit of joint actions with the organs of the JNA.'[95] Delimustafić would nevertheless prevent the arrest of Serb paramilitaries and the apprehension of their weapons, even while he arrested and disarmed members of the PL.[96] Halilović argues that had the MUP's forces been mobilised against the Serbian forces from the start of the war, its outcome would have been very different.[97] The MUP entered the war wholly unprepared for its role in the country's defence.[98] On the other hand Efendić, who commanded the ARBiH in April-May 1992, claims that Delimustafić provided the latter with vital military information gleaned via his connections with the JNA, helped arm and feed the fledgling Bosnian armed forces in the early weeks of the conflict and succeeded largely in dismantling the SDS barricades erected in Sarajevo in March 1992.[99] Delimustafić may have been collaborating with both sides out of uncertainty as to which would win the war.

Another questionable role in Bosnian defence preparations was played by Colonel Hazim Begović, an ethnic Muslim who served as Assistant Commander for Organisational-Mobilisational and Personal Affairs according to his own account, or according to other accounts Chief of the KOS for the 9th (Knin) Corps of the JNA until the end of 1990. At this time he moved to Sarajevo where he became Deputy Minister of Defence of Bosnia-Herzegovina. The newly elected Bosnian President Alija Izetbegović sought the advice of Army General Veljko Kadijević, Federal Secretary for People's Defence, on a suitable Muslim candidate for this post (the post of Bosnian Minister of Defence was to go to a Croat, Jerko Doko). Begović was appointed Deputy Minister of Defence of Bosnia-Herzegovina on Kadijević's advice.[100] During his tenure as a Bosnian government minister Begović pursued a policy of maximum military complacency and good relations with the JNA. In November 1991 he went on record as saying that 'so far as the armed forces of the SFRJ are concerned, the defence of Bosnia-Herzegovina is relatively well organised and I personally estimate that the security of Bosnia-Herzegovina is less under threat than that of neighbouring republics.' Begović was at this time without an apartment in Sarajevo and living in a JNA barracks.[101] He served as Deputy Minister of Defence until after the outbreak of war in Bosnia-Herzegovina in April 1992. During this period he entered into sharp conflict with his superior, Defence Minister Jerko Doko, accusing him of collaboration with the defence ministries of Croatia and Slovenia.[102] On 23 September 1991 Begović and two subordinates at the Bosnian Ministry of Defence, Under-secretary Ljubisav Terzić and Chief Republican Inspector Dragan Kapetina, accused Doko of maintaining secret consultations with the national defence minister of the Republic of Croatia through special telephone and other channels. They claimed that Doko was interested in preparations for the defence of Bosnia-Herzegovina 'only if they fit into the orders and policy of the Republic of Croatia and if they can result in effects which are aimed against Yugoslavia and the Yugoslav Army and create anti-Yugoslav and anti-Army sentiments among the public.' Both Terzić and Kapetina were members of the SDS.[103] Begović remained in his post until 9 April 1992 when he was removed by the Bosnian Presidency.[104] Consciously or not, his pro-JNA policy hindered preparations for the defence of the Republic of Bosnia-Herzegovina, which his fellow Knin Corps veterans were already working to destroy.

Bosnia-Herzegovina's defence preparations were hampered not only by outright treason, but by genuine confusion as to who was the enemy, fear of retaliation by the JNA and political splits among the defenders. The Sarajevo City Council of the SDA as late as May 1992 issued an order that 'the JNA not be provoked' since 'it will defend all the citizens of Bosnia-Herzegovina from every extremism. The JNA will not attack anyone, but it will defend itself; it will cooperate with all the peoples of Bosnia-Herzegovina in the struggle against terrorism and adventurism which arrive here from outside …' Efendić claims that thanks to their obedience to this order, the SDA-run municipal authorities of Hadžići in Sarajevo failed to organise resistance to the JNA, which consequently occupied the municipality without resistance on 8 May.[105] Likewise Halilović claims that the 25 February 1992 plan to destroy the bridges on the Drina was blocked by local Muslim leaders.[106] Muslim political leaders in Zvornik refused to cooperate with the PL, in the belief that the JNA would protect the Muslim community and that any covert military activity on the part of the latter would destroy inter-ethnic harmony.[107] In the preparations for the war, the Muslims and those committed to Bosnia-Herzegovina thus generally suffered from the disadvantages of not believing war would happen and of trusting in the JNA as a nationally impartial force, while the Serb and Croat nationalist sides were not hampered by any such illusions.

The Tuzla Municipal Council headed by Mayor Selim Bešlagić was a bulwark of Bosnian military and political resistance; the Tuzla-based 2nd Corps became the largest in the Bosnian Army. Nevertheless, PL officer Salim Hodžić claims that even after the outbreak of full scale war in April 1992 the municipal council and police harassed PL units in Tuzla, forcing them repeatedly to change bases, arresting their members and eventually on 23 April expelling them from municipal territory. The authorities of the neighbouring municipalities of Lukavac and Srebrenik likewise refused entry to the PL units, which eventually found protection with the authorities of Živinice municipality. Hodžić says that the Tuzla PL was nevertheless aided and equipped by officers of the TO and Secretariat for People's Defence in Tuzla.[108] Vahid Karavelić, another PL officer and later commander of the Sarajevo-based 1st Corps, accuses the Tuzla and Lukavac authorities of obstruction of the PL's movements, arrest of its members, unwillingness in assisting in the defence and liberation of neighbouring municipalities, refusal to attach the Bosnian state emblem to personnel uniforms and refusal to collaborate in disarming local JNA garrisons.[109] Karavelić was appointed TO commander for the Tuzla okrug on 13 April but his authority was not accepted by the Tuzla administration. According to Karavelić, 'At the time many could not grasp that Tuzla, and the whole of that area, had to be defended on the Drina and not in the Tuzla suburbs.'[110]

The perspective of Bešlagić's Tuzla administration was somewhat different. Bešlagić reported to the MUP in Sarajevo on 21 April that the Tuzla Municipal Council was active in mobilising and attempting to arm TO and militia forces, and on 22 April the council appointed a new commander for the TO Municipal Staff.[111] Bešlagić headed an administration of the Alliance of Reform Forces, subsequently the Union of Bosnian-Herzegovinian Social Democrats, which organised its resistance independently of the PL. Bešlagić's administration, representing as it did a multi-national political tradition that had evolved from Titoism and that was acceptable to most of Tuzla's citizens, achieved an unprecedented degree of unity in defensive measures between municipal council, TO and MUP. The defenders of Tuzla initially fought under the emblem of the city rather than of Bosnia-Herzegovina, which Bešlagić claims made possible a unified citizens' defence; when they later adopted the new Bosnian state emblem, a large number of Serbs deserted.[112] From Bešlagić's viewpoint, the activities of Karavelić's essentially Muslim and anti-Communist PL could only disrupt this unity and confuse the defenders. The PL operated outside the traditional framework of government and Karavelić himself was not a local Tuzla man. This mutual suspicion between the Tuzla Crisis Staff deriving from the Social Democratic municipal administration and the TO okrug command deriving from the PL would initially hamper the defence of north-east Bosnia.[113] Nevertheless, when on 7 April 1992 Serb policemen in Tuzla took advantage of the absence of their Muslim colleagues during the Bajram religious holiday to raid the offices of the Tuzla SDA headquarters, the event brought the Tuzla SDA and the Social Democratic administration of Tuzla together, producing Bosnia-Herzegovina's most solid regional defence.[114] The fissure between PL and TO occurred throughout government-controlled Bosnia-Herzegovina. The political history of the Bosnian Army from April 1992 is above all that of how the contradictions were resolved between the TO as a military institution and the PL as a military organisation; between the multi-national Bosnian state and its increasingly Muslim-national government.

TWO

Foundation of the Bosnian Army, 1992

Patriotic League and Territorial Defence

The Bosnian government stumbled reluctantly into a state of war as the reality of the aggression could no longer be avoided. At the end of March 1992 a meeting was held of members of the PL, TO and MUP at the Municipal Council of Stari Grad in Sarajevo, with the aim of uniting their forces under the leadership of the PL.[1] On 3–4 April, in response to the flight of Muslim refugees from already occupied north-eastern Bosnia and under pressure from members of his Presidency, Izetbegović permitted the municipalities to mobilise their TO forces according to their own discretion. In response, the two SDS members resigned from the Bosnian Presidency, and the following morning SDS paramilitary forces attacked the police academy at Vraca in Sarajevo as the first stage of their assault on the capital. From Vraca and from the SDS headquarters in the Holiday Inn hotel Serb snipers fired on a peace demonstration called that day in Sarajevo, and the independence of the SRBiH was proclaimed.[2] On 5–6 April Vukosavljević and his collaborators finally abandoned the headquarters of the TO, after stealing a large part of its military documents.[3] On 6 April, as Bosnia-Herzegovina's independence was recognised by the international community, the JNA occupied Sarajevo airport. On the

10th, JNA shelling knocked out the TV relay station on Hum, in the centre of Sarajevo, halting television and radio emissions in the city. The remaining, loyal members of the Bosnian TO Staff met on 6 April formally to suspend Vukosavljević from his duties. Nevertheless, members of the PL, unaware of the change in control of the TO Staff or continuing to view it as a hostile body, on 6 April invaded the premises of three of its subordinate staffs, those of the Okrug and City of Sarajevo and of the Centar Municipality, and seized weapons and communications equipment in what Sarajevo TO Commander Efendić describes as an 'act of plunder'. This action apparently frightened Vukosavljević and his fellow SDS officers from the TO Staff into taking refuge with General Kukanjac's JNA headquarters. At the same time, it brought the two principal Bosnian military forces, the PL and the TO, to the verge of armed conflict.[4]

Thirteen veterans of the Republican Staff of the Bosnian TO met at the Presidency Building in Sarajevo on 8 April to select a new TO Commander. As a result of its deliberations, the Bosnian Presidency dissolved the former TO Staff and appointed a new staff consisting of the Muslim Hasan Efendić as Commander and the Croat Stjepan Šiber as Chief of Staff; the Serb Jovan Divjak was subsequently appointed Deputy Commander. Efendić had not been the first choice for Commander; the post was first offered to the PL officer Rifat Bilajac, who refused it; it was thereupon offered to Šiber, who accepted, but Izetbegović rejected this because he wanted the Commander to be a Muslim. It was then decided that the Muslim Abdulah Kajević be appointed Commander and Šiber Chief of Staff, but this was rejected by Šiber on the grounds that Kajević was younger and lower-ranking than himself. Finally, Efendić was chosen as an ethnic Muslim who was older in years and equal in rank to Šiber.[5] Šiber claims that Efendić was selected on his recommendation, as an experienced and competent ethnic-Muslim officer of appropriate rank and age, and that he also suggested that Jovan Divjak be included in the staff.[6] At the same time the Presidency became the Supreme Command, while the Republican TO Staff remained subordinate to the Ministry for People's Defence. The 'Republican Staff of the Territorial Defence of the

Socialist Republic of Bosnia-Herzegovina' was renamed the 'Staff of the Territorial Defence of the Republic of Bosnia-Herzegovina'; forty-eight out of the eighty-five members of the old staff pledged their loyalty to the new, including a handful of Serbs – all but one of whom, however, deserted the Staff immediately afterwards and left Sarajevo for Pale or Belgrade. The sole exception was Divjak, who as Deputy Commander was to make a crucial contribution to the organisation of the new army. By contrast, virtually all the Croat and Muslim staff members pledged their loyalty to the new staff. At the same Presidency meeting, an adaption of the coat-of-arms of the medieval Bosnian King Tvrtko (a blue shield with six *fleurs-de-lis*) was chosen as Bosnia-Herzegovina's provisional emblem of state. The new Staff then secured a pledge of loyalty in the struggle for Bosnian independence from the Staff of the Sarajevo City TO and seventy-two other municipal- and county-level TO Staffs. Commander Efendić immediately paid a visit to PL Commander Sefer Halilović, whose Staff was located immediately to the north of the Presidency Building in the Sarajevo ward of Bjelave; according to Halilović, he had to give his approval of the new appointments. Also on 8 April the Presidency declared a state of war-danger, something that was a step lower than a full declaration of a state of war, which was avoided largely to avoid alienating international public opinion by appearing too aggressive. Finally, on the same day, the Socialist Republic of Bosnia-Herzegovina dropped the word 'Socialist' from its name, becoming simply the 'Republic of Bosnia-Herzegovina'. On 9 April the Presidency declared the unification of all armed forces on the territory of Bosnia-Herzegovina, with a deadline of 15 April for all existing armed units to accept this decision.[7] In addition to the PL and TO, these included the forces of the MUP (then the most powerful armed force under Bosnian government command), the SDA 'Green Berets' militia, the HVO, and the 'Croatian Armed Forces' (HOS – the militia of the Croatian Party of Rights, which advocated the incorporation of the whole of Bosnia-Herzegovina in a Great Croatia).[8] Together they comprised the Armed Forces of the Republic of Bosnia-Herzegovina (OS RBiH).

The Bosnian state and its armed forces in April 1992 were doubly divided: not only did the OS RBiH encompass a medley of military forces with separate structures and different political agendas, but members of each of them from the head of state to the grass-roots level were still vacillating between resistance to and collaboration with Serbia and the JNA. Members of the Bosnian Presidency included waverers and outright traitors; the PL and TO were still in rivalry; the MUP forces remained not fully integrated into the OS RBiH; officers defecting from the JNA were mistrusted as double agents, sometimes rightly; individual military units frequently acted in an independent, undisciplined and sometimes criminal manner; and the entire apparatus of state, army and government was riddled with KOS agents, Croat and Serb nationalists, pure criminals and others each pursuing their own political or personal agendas. This was at a time when the overt Serbian military conquest of Bosnian territory was beginning with a seemingly inexorable blitzkrieg; the 'unoccupied' part of the country, including the capital, was still studded with JNA garrisons; the HVO was organising as a separate military force whose leaders were plotting to stab the Bosnian resistance in the back at the right moment; and the Western powers appeared to have sanctioned the partition of Bosnia-Herzegovina in advance.[9] The extent to which the Presidency's orders regarding the new army would have results at the local level depended upon local military conditions. Thus on 10 April the Okrug TO Staff for Bihać informed the Republican Staff that whereas the TO staffs of the predominantly Muslim municipalities of Bihać, Velika Kladuša, Cazin and Bosanska Krupa had unanimously accepted the new TO command at the Republican level, those of the predominantly Serb municipalities of Bosansko Grahovo, Bosanski Petrovac and Drvar refused to do so. Ethnically mixed municipalities tended to remain passive in the forlorn hope of avoiding conflict. The municipal assembly in Modriča, under Muslim and Croat control, on 14 April rejected the idea of mobilising the TO for fear that this would worsen relations with local Serbs; the municipality was therefore easily overrun by Serbian forces soon after the start of the war. By contrast the Srebrenica municipality took active steps to prepare resistance and was able to hold out until 1995.[10]

Bosnia-Herzegovina was still at this point a multi-national state and the organisation of its armed forces reflected this. As we have seen, the Republican TO Staff appointed by the Presidency on 8 April had a Muslim Commander, a Serb Deputy Commander and a Croat Chief of Staff. According to the 'Law of the Armed Forces of the Republic of Bosnia-Herzegovina' published in 20 May 1992 the OS RBiH were defined as 'the common armed forces of all citizens and nations of the Republic – Muslims, Serbs and Croats and members of other nations and nationalities who live in it', while the HVO was defined as a constituent part of the ARBiH.[11] The equality of the Latin and Cyrillic alphabets was guaranteed.[12] One official handbook of the OS RBiH General Staff published in 1992 printed three examples of its military emblems named after three historical figures: the Croat 'King Tomislav'; the Muslim 'Dragon of Bosnia [Husein Kapetan Gradaščević]' and the Serb 'Radomir Putnik'.[13] The Statute on Military Service enacted by the Presidency on 23 June stated that 'military duty is an inalienable part of the rights and duties of citizens of the Republic of Bosnia-Herzegovina to defend the homeland and safeguard their freedom, independence, sovereignty and territorial unity and the social order guaranteed by the constitution of the Republic.'[14] The oath of loyalty required of Bosnian soldiers, according to the Presidency decision of eight days later, was: 'I pledge to defend the independence, sovereignty and unity of the Republic of Bosnia-Herzegovina; that I shall in a conscientious and disciplined manner carry out all tasks and duties of a member of the Army of the Republic of Bosnia-Herzegovina; and that I shall defend its freedom and honour and be steadfast in that struggle.'[15]

The Bosnian Army in the summer of 1992 was organised according to the principle of a nation of citizens with equal duties and loyalties regardless of nationality. At the start of the war the Bosnian Army was 20% Serb and Croat, while the General Staff was 18 or 20% Croat and 12% Serb.[16] This multi-nationality of the Bosnian Army was in some sense ornamental, in that Serb and Croat soldiers from the rank and file up to Deputy Commander Divjak himself were not trusted by their superiors or by the regime.[17] Nevertheless, it was a multi-nationality that provided a basis that could have been built on to form a truly multi-national liberation struggle. Whether this would occur would depend on the internal political evolution of the ARBiH. According to Mirko Pejanović, a Serb member of the wartime Bosnian Presidency, the new commander of the ARBiH was a champion of the multi-national principle: 'I believed that Sefer Halilović was very firm in his view of the principles of the Army of Bosnia-Herzegovina, which was that it was an armed force of all its citizens and all its peoples and that it was a multi-ethnic and multi-national force; a force made up of different nations.'[18] One aspect that reflected the intended multi-national character of the ARBiH was the Administration for Morale, an institution promoted by Halilović in collaboration with the Serb members of the Presidency, Pejanović and Nenad Kecmanović. The Administration for Morale recruited politicians, intellectuals and other public figures of all nationalities and political persuasions whose task it was to mobilise the Bosnian population behind the war effort. This institution, however, never assumed an important role and gradually lost any importance as Bosnian state politics became increasingly dominated by the SDA and the HDZ to the exclusion of all broader and more civic-oriented currents.[19] Even among the supporters of a multi-national army there was disagreement over how it should be organised, for the question was raised of whether Serbs and Croats should have their own distinct military units within the Army, or whether by contrast the Army should simply enrol citizens regardless of their nationality. Defence Minister Jerko Doko advised members of the Presidency in the summer of 1992 to form a 'Serb Defence Council', an idea that was also favoured around the same time by 1st Corps commander Mustafa Hajrulahović-Talijan. However, Presidency Member Pejanović disagreed, favouring instead the ARBiH as the homogenous army of all the citizens of Bosnia-Herzegovina.[20] In the event no separate Serb military units or structures were established within the ARBiH, except briefly and on a small scale in the Tuzla region as described below, while the multi-ethnic composition of the ARBiH would not survive the war. The price of political unity and military recovery according to the political programme of the SDA would be the irreparable fracturing of Bosnia-Herzegovina's fragile multi-national unity.

The split between the PL and the TO was not immediately resolved with the changes of 8–9 April. Efendić was a professional officer schooled in the Titoist military and ideological tradition, for whom the shift from serving the 'Socialist Republic of Bosnia-Herzegovina' to serving the independent 'Republic of Bosnia-Herzegovina' represented no kind of professional break. He was also, as he says, a 'declared atheist'.[21] Efendić claims that, upon being offered the post of TO commander for Bosnia-Herzegovina by President Izetbegović and Defence Minister Doko, he asked them 'Will our army be multi-national or uni-national? If it will be uni-national I do not want to be commander.' He accepted the post only when he was assured that the army would be multi-national. He thereupon gave a speech to the other members of the TO Staff in which he compared the contemporary situation in Bosnia-Herzegovina to that of 1941, when the Ustasha regime attempted to destroy the Serbs as a people and the Partisans waged a guerrilla war in response.[22] Efendić was the protégé of the Bosnian Minister of Finance Hasan Čengić, via whom he received his instructions from Izetbegović. He nevertheless remained the object of suspicion on the part of some members of the PL, who represented a different, dissident tradition. Halilović and his General Staff refused to turn over the PL's intelligence and organisational archive to Efendić and the TO Republican Staff. Halilović subsequently claimed the PL did not have confidence in the officers of the TO, including Efendić himself, whose Serb wife was living at the time in Serbia. Halilović also believed that the PL and not the TO should have been made the framework for the OS RBiH, with the TO being subsumed in the PL rather than vice versa. Other PL officers reacted against being included in TO staffs. Efendić and Šiber, by contrast, claimed that TO staffs were better organised and trained than their PL counterparts, although the PL commanded greater manpower. Efendić further claims in his memoirs that in some okrugs, such as Bihać and Zenica, the PL scarcely existed in a militarily credible form and it was the TO alone that formed the basis for the ARBiH.[23] Despite this dispute, the PL General Staff was formally moved to the Presidency Building on 12 April and Halilović was appointed Chief of the Operational Centre at the TO Republican Staff. The functional PL General Staff, however, remained at Bjelave. On 10 April, two PL officers were appointed to leading positions in the Ministry of Defence. One of these, Munib Bišić, replaced Hazim Begović as Deputy Minister of Defence.[24]

The Republican Staff of the TO formally assumed command of all units formed on the political platform of the PL on 15 April – the day marks the official birth of the ARBiH.[25] According to Efendić, there were 91,243 troops officially registered in the new TO by 24 April, with the true figure considerably higher.[26] Nevertheless, this formal unification of the Bosnian armed forces did not resolve the structural and ideological divisions that remained between its different wings. When on 18 April Efendić ordered the formation of platoons, companies, detachments and battalions for the TO, it resulted in a clash with Halilović, who argued that they already existed.[27] Such was the beginning of the long-running conflict between Čengić and Halilović that would ultimately end with the latter's dismissal – a continuation, in some sense, of the conflict between the Bosnian state and the PL, even though Čengić was himself a founding member of the latter. For while the SDA and PL leaderships had begun as two halves of the same political movement, the assumption by Izetbegović and Čengić of leadership of the Republic put them in a position of needing to reconcile the country's conflicting political forces and traditions. The political agenda of the SDA leadership would therefore diverge from that of the PL command. At the ground level, meanwhile, there remained the division between the PL and the TO and, more broadly, between on the one hand those officers of the OS RBiH who had held similar posts under the old regime and remained broadly 'Titoist' in outlook and on the other the genuine Muslim nationalists, hostile to the old order and seeking radical change. Thus the SDA mayor of the Stari Grad municipality of Sarajevo, Selim Hadžibajrić repeatedly clashed with Efendić over the organisation of local defences. According to Efendić, during a meeting of local TO commanders Hadžibajrić criticised him for using the expression 'Good evening', on the grounds that he had no right to be TO commander if he did not use the correct Islamic greeting 'Salam aleikum'. Efendić responded that not everyone present at the meeting was a Muslim. Efendić claims further that Hadžibajrić enjoyed a close relationship with the local Green Berets militia, to which he gave free reign systematically to rob local shops and businesses. The stolen goods, allegedly taken for the needs of the city's defence, ended up in private hoards of members of the Green Berets.[28]

The Bosnian police, under the MUP, was another important force at the disposal of the Bosnian leadership whose integration into the OS RBiH posed problems for the Bosnian leadership. The active and reserve police-forces, at 30,000 and 20,000 policemen respectively, together comprised the single most powerful component of the OS RBiH. On 4 April 1992 when the Presidency ordered the general mobilisation of the TO, the MUP forces were put under TO command, and their units played a key role in the defence of Sarajevo. MUP Special Forces commander Dragan Vikić was appointed to head the Sarajevo defences. On 5–6 April the MUP Special Forces were defeated by the JNA in a battle for the Vraca police academy, but in mid-April they defeated an advance into the Sarajevo ward of Grbavica by the Serbian 'White Eagles' – henceforth known as the 'White Chickens'.[29] Nevertheless, the MUP under Delimustafić continued after the declaration of independence to act more as an instrument of Belgrade's rule over Bosnia-Herzegovina than as an institution of Bosnian statehood, and prevented the police's full mobilisation in the latter's defence.[30] This problem for the Bosnian leadership would not be overcome until the events in Sarajevo of 5–6 May.

Finally, a potentially valuable human resource at the disposal of Bosnia-Herzegovina's defenders was the Partisan veterans of World War II, organised in the 'Union of Associated Fighters of the People's Liberation War', to which name the word 'Antifascist' was subsequently added, making it the 'Union of Associated Fighters of the People's Liberation Antifascist War' (SUBNOAR). Despite their advanced years they often possessed considerable military expertise, some having been high-ranking generals during the Tito era. On 9 April 1992 the Bosnian daily *Oslobođenje* published a condemnation of the Serbian attack on Sarajevo by a number of high-ranking Bosnian Partisan veterans of all nationalities. On 3 June 1992 a number of high-ranking Partisan veterans published another statement in which they offered their services to the Republic of Bosnia-Herzegovina and its defence. The SDA leadership and the

PL for ideological reasons had little interest in drawing upon the Partisan veterans, but were not averse in principle to their involvement. The Serb members of the Bosnian Presidency, Nenad Kecmanović and Mirko Pejanović, suggested that certain high-ranking former Partisan commanders should be enlisted in the leadership of the ARBiH. Izetbegović gave his consent to the proposal and Kecmanović and Pejanović held talks with three retired JNA generals and Partisan veterans, Džemil Šarac, Mirko Vranić and Milan Ačić, proposing to them that Šarac be appointed Commander of the General Staff of the ARBiH and Vranić and Ačić his deputies. Although all three gave their blessing to the new army, they refused to join it, citing their advanced years.[31] Eventually on 24 June the top commanders of the ARBiH met with a larger group of retired JNA generals, the majority of whom were Partisan veterans, to discuss their possible cooperation with the war effort. Indicative of the barriers to cooperation is the fact that the Bosnian commanders on this occasion denounced the JNA generals, whom they blamed for the war.[32] Nevertheless Šarac, Vranić and Ačić were included within a 'Military Council' formed on 7 July 1992 as an advisory body attached to the General Staff of the ARBiH.[33] This body, that included leading statesmen such as the Prime Minister and Interior Minister, proved to be a token body with no influence on the course of events. The three Partisan veterans only ever attended two sessions of the Council.[34]

Izetbegović himself was not averse, however, to drawing on the Partisan legacy in his propaganda. On 24 November 1993 he proclaimed that 'Today in Bosnia we once again have scenes from World War II ... Then there were Chetniks and Ustashas. Now they are once again on the scene. Only worse Chetniks than those Chetniks, worse Ustashas than those Ustashas ... Now the question is asked: where is the third side ? Then the third side was the Partisans. Today there is also a third side. That is our national Bosnian Army, which does not have that ideological, Communist motif; which is democratic.' Izetbegović claimed that unlike the Chetniks and Ustashas the Partisans 'did not kill women and children. They won because of that. We must remember this well and draw from it the message: We shall win if we earn the reputation of an army that does not kill women and children.'[35] Izetbegović was head of a regime that combined the traditions of both the Partisans and their Muslim autonomist opponents. Although the Partisan legacy became less relevant to the regime as the war progressed, it never wholly disappeared from view. Meanwhile SUBNOAR and many famous individual Bosnian Partisan veterans of all nationalities remained loyal to the Bosnian state and its war-effort and made public statements in their support.[36]

The Question of the Yugoslav People's Army

A much greater danger to Bosnia-Herzegovina's security than the TO-PL division, though in some sense related to it, was the Presidency's continued belief that it could avoid conflict with the JNA. On 11 April Efendić published in the national daily *Oslobođenje* an appeal to the JNA in Bosnia-Herzegovina to establish a joint command with the TO, in the hope that the JNA could be included within the OS RBiH. The Presidency demanded that acting Yugoslav Federal Secretary of Defence Blagoje Adžić come to Sarajevo to resolve the JNA's status. Negotiations over the JNA's status in Bosnia-Herzegovina would continue until its final withdrawal from Sarajevo in June. This had the effect of tying the TO's hands in its combat with the JNA. On 12–13 April Deputy Commander Divjak and Kadir Jušić drew up a plan for the defence and liberation of Bosnia-Herzegovina, which involved the disarming of JNA garrisons on Bosnian-government territory. On 14 April Efendić faxed the plan to each of the seventy-three local TO staffs. These steps were taken without consultation with the Presidency or the HDZ-controlled Ministry of Defence. So poor was Bosnian security at this time that seventy-three faxes of the plan simultaneously arrived at Radovan Karadžić's office at Pale. In the resulting furore General Milutin Kukanjac, commander of the Sarajevo-based 2nd Military District, accused Efendić of declaring war on the JNA. Izetbegović was forced publicly to disassociate himself from the plan and to state that Efendić had exceeded his authority.[37]

Izetbegović signed an agreement with Belgrade representative Branko Kostić on 26 April for the withdrawal of the JNA from Bosnia-Herzegovina along with both its own weapons and those it had confiscated from the TO.[38] This was bitterly opposed by Halilović, who had begun to organise the blockade of the nine JNA garrisons in Sarajevo with a view to their seizure and disarmament.[39] Izetbegović similarly vetoed the plan of Halilović and his fellow PL officer Rifat Bilajac to seize the confiscated TO weapons at the JNA warehouse at Faletići, on the north-east corner of Sarajevo, for fear of JNA retaliation against the city. The JNA was allowed to withdraw the weapons from Faletići, yet retaliated anyway. Efendić subsequently claimed that the PL was too weak and disorganised to have successfully seized the weapons; he criticises the sectarian unwillingness of the PL officers to enlist the aid of himself and the TO in the seizure of the weapons, but also the vacillation and cowardice of the Bosnian political leadership, which was unwilling to do anything that might offend the JNA or the Serbian authorities.[40] Izetbegović ordered the JNA's withdrawal from Bosnia-Herzegovina only on 27 April. On 29 April Efendić issued an order for systematic attacks by the TO on JNA forces, which once again fell into the hands of the Pale Serb leadership, which used it to claim once again that the Bosnian leadership had declared war on the JNA. Once again the Bosnian Presidency rebuked Efendić for this alleged provocation.[41] General Divjak, writing after the war and his own retirement, has described Izetbegović and the Bosnian political leadership in these days as guilty of 'defeatist behaviour' and of 'incompetence and superficial knowledge and monitoring of the military and political situation', for 'How else to describe the early assessments of the situation by those in responsible positions in the government? First, that there would be no war in Bosnia-Herzegovina; then that while it was possible that war would break out, it could never do so in Sarajevo; after which they said that an agreement would be reached with the JNA to transform part of that force into the TO of the Republic of Bosnia-Herzegovina !'.[42] For a competent professional former JNA officer like Divjak the last of these aspirations was particularly laughable.

Nevertheless, Izetbegović's stance towards the JNA would harden following the events of 2–3 May, described below.

The JNA could not be transformed into a Bosnian army, nor could it be split along local lines as could the TO. Individual officers could, however, be peeled off. On 13 April Efendić issued a new appeal for JNA officers to put themselves at the disposal of the defence of Bosnia-Herzegovina. It was only then that the men who would come to dominate the ARBiH were to join it: Rasim Delić answered the summons the same day, and Fikret Muslimović two days later. Delić, who was later to become commander of the ARBiH, remained in the JNA until 12–13 April in the hope that the JNA's status could be resolved within the framework of the Bosnian state.[43] The recruitment of these JNA officers on the part of the Bosnian government was a double-edged sword, for while the ARBiH needed trained officers, there could not be absolute confidence in the loyalty of the new arrivals. Enver Hadžihasanović, the commander of the 49th Brigade of the JNA at Lukavica to the south of Sarajevo, answered the summons on 17 April and was appointed to command the TO at Ilidža during the decisive battle for this key western suburb of the capital. This in practice meant that officers who had up till then belonged to an occupying force were now at the head of the country's defences. Sead Delić, who answered Efendić's summons in April and would become commander of the Bosnian Army's 2nd Corps in December 1994, had fought as a JNA officer against the Croats at Varaždin in September 1991, for which he was decorated for bravery in Belgrade.[44] Rasim Delić, who in April 1992 became Chief of the Instructional-Operational Organ of the TO Republican Staff and in June 1993 would replace Halilović at the helm of the ARBiH, had up to 13 April been Chief of the Operational Department of the Sarajevo Corps of the JNA.[45] At the time of Delić's appointment as Commander, the demoted Halilović would accuse him of having helped prepare the Serbian siege of Sarajevo from the JNA's Zlatište base on Mt Trebević.[46] Members of Sarajevo's Green Berets have accused Delić of having been captured by Bosnian forces when his car broke down on Trebević and forcibly included in the TO. Delić, however, claims that the Zlatište base was effectively a place of exile for Ante Karanušić, the Croat Chief of Staff of the JNA's Sarajevo Corps, and for other non-Serb JNA officers who were not permitted to know of or participate in the plans of the JNA concerning Sarajevo.[47] Almost all of the most senior officers of the ARBiH came out of the JNA; some, such as Halilović and Karavelić, were founders of the PL. Croatian sources accused Halilović himself – falsely, it later transpired – of having participated in the JNA's destruction of the Croatian town of Vukovar. They similarly accused the spectacularly successful Atif Dudaković, commander of the ARBiH's 5th Corps, of having bombarded the Croatian town of Zadar while in the JNA.[48] At all events, there does appear to have been a certain gulf between those who left the JNA earlier to participate in the PL and those who joined Bosnia-Herzegovina's defenders only after the aggression had begun.

There would subsequently be three currents within the new Bosnian Army: the officers of the PL, the officers of the TO, and the new arrivals from the JNA.[49] Muslimović would in June 1992 complain of the hostility within the TO directed against the newcomers and subsequently accuse PL officers of a sectarian attitude towards former JNA officers, on whose supposed treachery they blamed their own military defeats.[50] According to Muslimović, accusations of disloyalty levelled against him and other former JNA officers were inspired by Great Serbian and Croatian propaganda aimed at sowing dissension in Bosnia-Herzegovina's defenders and thus sabotaging the emergence of a Bosnian army.[51] Similarly, Divjak has written of the negative effect on the war effort of a policy whereby, out of mistrust, trained former JNA officers were squandered as rank-and-file soldiers while politically trusted men with no military training or experience were put in command of large military units.[52] As we shall see, the changes associated with the replacement of Halilović in June 1993 may have been in part a clash between the PL and the newcomers from the JNA. Izetbegović may have ultimately preferred the latter as they lacked the autonomous local bases of support of their PL counterparts and were therefore more dependent on the President's patronage. Furthermore, torn as they had been between professional loyalty to the JNA and patriotic loyalty to Bosnia-Herzegovina, the newcomers' political and moral equivocation closely resembled that of Izetbegović himself, who still wavered between a political agreement with the JNA and military resistance to it. By contrast, the PL officers' straightforward enmity toward the JNA was out of keeping with government policy.

The Croat Defence Council

The HVO, as the Bosnian Croat counterpart to the Patriotic League, was formally founded on 8 April 1992 and consisted of about 132,000 troops. It was to make an important contribution to Bosnia-Herzegovina's defences at the start of the war, but ultimately its organisational structure, the ideology of its leaders and their loyalty to the Tuđman regime in Zagreb were to lead it into rebellion and conflict with the ARBiH. The experience of the Serbian aggression against Croatia in 1991 had led Bosnian Croats generally to begin preparations for their own resistance earlier than their Muslim neighbours. The Croat inclination toward autonomous armed organisation was heightened by the Serbian aggression against Croatia during 1991, the Serbian preparation for an attack on Bosnia-Herzegovina during early 1992 and the failure of the Bosnian government and Muslim politicians in general to take sides against the former or to take steps to resist the latter. Bosnian Croats, particularly Herzegovinians, fought in their thousands in Croatia's war of independence. In April 1992, following the outbreak of full-scale war in Bosnia-Herzegovina, Herzegovinian Croats were reported as commonly saying that 'the war for us began long before: last summer, in Croatia!'.[53] Inhabitants of Bosnian Croat villages and towns engaged in actions aimed at blocking JNA movements against Croatia, while JNA troops attacked their villages, destroyed the Bosnian Croat village of Ravno, fired on civilians in Višegrad and went on a looting spree against Croat and Muslim homes in Trebinje, all prior to the outbreak of full-scale war in April 1992 and without provoking serious condemnation from the Bosnian government. In November 1991, two Bosnian Croat regional political bodies were set up, the 'Croat Community of Bosanska Posavina' in northern Bosnia and the 'Croat Community of Herzeg-

Bosna' (HZ H-B), the latter based in the small town of Grude in Herzegovina. The 'Croat Community of Bosanska Posavina' was set up on 12 November, six days before the HZ H-B, which may have been due to the greater military threat faced by the Posavina Croats from the JNA.[54] These moves unified the already established Bosnian Croat regional associations and, at least in the case of the HZ H-B, had as their goal the formation of a Great Croatian state. Thus the foundation of the HZ H-B was preceded by a meeting of the presidencies of the Crisis Staffs of the Herzegovinian and Travnik Regional Communities on 12 November, attended by leading HDZ figures including Dario Kordić, Vladimir Šoljić, Božo Rajić and others, who declared their aim to be 'the realisation of our age-old dream – a common Croatian state'. The 'proclamation of a Croatian banovina in Bosnia-Herzegovina' was to be followed by 'the holding of a referendum for annexation to the Republic of Croatia …' They condemned the idea of a 'non-existent sovereign Bosnia-Herzegovina' in which 'the Croat nation would be condemned to genocide and historical disappearance'.[55]

Like their Serb counterparts in the SDS, HDZ bodies had utilised the existing local TO and police structures to establish military units throughout Bosnia-Herzegovina where Croats lived, that also recruited many Muslims and even some Serbs.[56] In Kiseljak, whose pre-war population was approximately 52% Croat and 41% Muslim, the HVO was formed when Croat officers seceded from the TO municipal staff soon after the start of the war and set up their own staff.[57] In 1992 the Serbian offensive aimed to drive a wedge between the Croats in Western Herzegovina and those in Central Bosnia, so as to surround the Bosnian heartland and threaten southern Croatia.[58] On 8 April, the JNA captured Kupres, a southern Bosnian town with a substantial Croat population that guarded the gateway to Central Bosnia.[59] The inadequacy of the Bosnian government's defence preparations left the initiative for defence in the hands of local Croat leaders. The HVO fought under the *šahovnica*, the Croat national symbol, but it attracted many Muslims eager to resist, as did the HOS, the military wing of the Croatian Party of Rights, which advocated the unification of Croatia and Bosnia-Herzegovina in a Great-Croatian state. Furthermore, in the initial stages of the war a degree of cooperation was possible between the HVO and the ARBiH. According to the former president of the SDA in Mostar, Ismet Hadžiosmanović, the HDZ and HVO gave 'unselfish' support to the military preparations of the PL in the Herzegovinian capital, supplying it with weapons imported from Croatia. The SDA and the HDZ in Mostar organised the defence of the town together.[60] The Mostar HVO at this time had a Muslim commander, Jasmin Jaganjac, who had served as an officer in the Croatian Army in 1991. The HVO in Bosanski Brod included Muslims among its commanders up until the time of its fall to Serb forces in October 1992.[61]

The Bosnian government, itself a coalition that included the HDZ, viewed the HVO as a legitimate component of the OS RBiH. The HDZ held key posts in the Bosnian government, including the premiership (Jure Pelivan) and the Ministry of Defence (Jerko Doko). The HDZ leadership, however, although paying lip-service to the legitimacy and territorial integrity of Bosnia-Herzegovina, in practice pursued its own policy, hampering defence at the all-Bosnian level while building up autonomous Bosnian Croat forces in areas earmarked for inclusion in the projected Bosnian Croat state. Defence Minister Doko had advocated the TO's mobilisation already in September 1991, in order to assist Croatia's war effort.[62] However, both Pelivan and Doko were essentially hostile to the Bosnian TO, viewing it as an anti-Croat force equivalent to the JNA. This HDZ hostility further paralysed as a Bosnian defence force the TO, already gravely weakened by the activities of Vukosavljević's SDS-controlled TO Staff.[63] Following the Presidency's declaration of the unification of Bosnia-Herzegovina's armed forces on 9 April, Doko stated that the HVO was 'his business' and that he would take care of its incorporation in the OS RBiH. The HZ H-B responded to the Presidency's order for the unification of all armed forces in Bosnia-Herzegovina with a formal statement on 24 April, in which it rejected the proposition that the HVO should be absorbed within the Bosnian TO and reaffirmed the HVO's existence as a separate armed force.[64] Doko proceeded to give the HVO priority in receiving armaments from factories in government hands. Thus all armaments from the 'Bratstvo' factory in Novi Travnik were delivered to municipalities where the HVO was strong, such as Busovača, Kiseljak and Vitez.[65] Halilović claims that Delimustafić likewise delivered 12,000 guns to the HVO in Western Herzegovina on the orders of the KOS Chief Vasiljević, for use against the ARBiH.[66] Such were the complexities of the political alliances within Bosnia-Herzegovina. The Croat Željko Knez was appointed commander of the Tuzla-based 2nd Corps, through the intervention of Mayor Bešlagić. He built up a predominantly Croat staff and, following his visit to President Tudman in Zagreb in late July, was accused of pursing a 'Croat' military strategy that gave priority to the liberation of Posavina at the expense of Srebrenica and East Bosnia; he was also made an honorary member of the HDZ.[67] Knez was dismissed in March 1993 for his failure to assist Bosnian forces in the Srebrenica and Vlasenica regions.[68]

The HVO was praised for its role in the defence of Sarajevo by 1st Corps commander Mustafa Hajrulahović-Talijan,[69] while Halilović in the same period lamented the role of unrepresentative extremists within the HVO, which he nevertheless spoke of warmly as the ARBiH's ally.[70] Tension was already apparent, however, in relations between the HVO and the ARBiH in Sarajevo; and in August 1992 the HVO commander in the Stup district of Sarajevo, Velimir Marić, accused the ARBiH of taking control of 'Croat positions' in Stup and issued an ultimatum for it to withdraw.[71] The ARBiH had spent the summer of 1992 attempting without success to subordinate to its command the Stup HVO, which obstructed all attempts at military cooperation, its officers instead engaging in embezzlement and black-marketeering.[72] By September Hajrulahović had lost his positive view of the HVO in Stup, accusing it of collaborating with the Serb besiegers.[73] That a general conflict between the two armies did not break out was because the policies of the Croatian leadership was at this point in time restrained. The HVO's status was confirmed by the Izetbegović-Tudman agreement in Zagreb of 21 July 1992, when the two Presidents agreed to form a joint staff of the ARBiH and the HVO. On account of the preoccupation of both leaders with securing international goodwill, the pact called for full military cooperation between their respective countries only if international efforts to end the war failed. Under international pressure Tuđman was at this stage soft-pedalling his anti-Bosnian policy.

The Serbian Blitzkrieg

Within a month of the Bosnian declaration of independence of 6 April 1992, political and military developments took place that would largely determine the course of the country's history during the following three and a half years of war. Despite their careful preparation and enormous superiority in weapons, the SDS and the VRS were inevitably stymied by their desire to secede from Bosnia-Herzegovina and conquer it at the same time; the political goal of a separate Bosnian Serb state clashed with the military goal of conquering as much territory as possible. The People's Liberation Movement had involved a majority-Serb Bosnian Partisan army entering and liberating Bosnian cities; in 1945 both the Bosnian Prime Minister and the secretary of the Bosnian Provincial Committee of the Communist Party were Serbs. Serbs at that time formed a plurality in the Bosnian population and were furthermore over-represented in the Bosnian bureaucracy: according to Lopušina they comprised 75% of Bosnian secret service officials during the first two decades of Communist rule.[74] They still enjoyed a plurality of posts in the Bosnian MUP in 1991, although there were now more Bosnian Muslims in the population as a whole.[75] 1992 was in a sense 1945 in reverse, with Serb officials under SDS direction abandoning the institutions of state and forming new, purely Serb local- and central-government bodies. This in practice meant surrendering the centres of power in the large cities to the non-Serb parties, most symbolically with the Serb Presidency members and parliamentary deputies abandoning Sarajevo to establish their capital in the suburb of Pale, a skiing resort. As a municipality subordinate to the city of Sarajevo, Pale had had Serb representatives in the organs of the Sarajevo city government. During the run up to the war these representatives had systematically looted the Sarajevo city organs of money, goods and weapons, which were relocated to Pale to assist in the establishment there of a Serb government. Several of these individuals, including Mićo Stanišić, Chief of the Sarajevo City MUP, and Nenad Veselinović (a member of a family that had been pro-Chetnik in World War II), secretary of the Sarajevo City Secretariat for Transport, then became dominant figures in the new Pale Serb government, with Stanišić becoming Minister of Internal Affairs of the Serb Republic.[76] SDS supporters in the MUP in March 1992 established their own separatist 'Serb MUP' which began functioning the following month in the Serb-held Vraca police academy.[77]

The interdependency of Bosnia-Herzegovina's peoples and regions was not recognised by Serb nationalism. This interdependency meant that for months after the start of the fighting the VRS's arms factory at Vogošća remained powered by the Sarajevo electricity grid while Serb homes in the Ozren region in the Serb Republic were throughout the war powered by Tuzla's generator at Kreka. Yet no attempt whatsoever was made by the SDS to appeal to sections of the non-Serb population of Bosnia-Herzegovina, and the JNA garrisons remained as islands in a Muslim and Croat sea. On 14 April the defenders of Sarajevo received the plan drawn up by Divjak and Jušić to break the siege of the city; the resulting offensive into Ilidža was halted by the JNA.[78] But the JNA and SDS could no more occupy Sarajevo than the defenders could break out; their inability to appeal politically to the capital's population made it impossible for them to establish their rule there or even to supply the JNA garrisons located in the city. Their failure in April and May to seize control of Bosnia's principal cities other than Banja Luka and Bijeljina, and their programme of expelling the non-Serb population from the territories they occupied, left them with an economically and demographically bankrupt territorial base from which to wage war. Conversely, the successful defence of Sarajevo and Tuzla against the Serbian attacks of early- and mid-May could be described as Bosnia-Herzegovina's Battle of the Marne, leaving the country's defenders with the demographically preponderant Bosnian heartland that would guarantee them an eventual military revival. The limitations in the Bosnian government's own political programme, however, placed limits on the extent of the latter.

The military forces headed by the SDS acted essentially as an adjunct to the regular and paramilitary forces of Belgrade – the JNA and JNA-led militias from Serbia proper, financed by the Serbian Interior Ministry. It was these that spearheaded the Serbian blitzkrieg, organised according to an adaptation of a plan originally designed to combat a prospective invasion by NATO of the Sarajevo area by way of the Croatian coast.[79] Bijeljina was attacked by the 'Tigers' of Željko Ražnjatović Arkan on 1 April and occupied by the JNA on 3 April. To the south, the East Bosnian town of Zvornik was attacked by the Tigers, the Chetniks of Vojislav Šešelj and the JNA's Užice Corps on 8 April and occupied on the 10th. Šešelj later recounted how his forces were subordinated to the JNA during this offensive.[80] Bijeljina and Zvornik together formed a hinge linking the Serbian-controlled territories in Bosanska Krajina to the west with those in Eastern Bosnia and Herzegovina to the south. A northern 'corridor' to Bosanska Krajina and to the Serb-held territories in Croatia beyond it was tenuously established in early May, with the conquest of Brčko, Derventa and Doboj. The latter two towns were captured by Serbian forces previously based in occupied Croatia. Large numbers of JNA troops withdrawn from Croatia had been stationed in Doboj, and played a decisive role in the Serbian conquest of the town on 3 May.[81] The south-west Bosnian town of Kupres fell to the JNA on 8 April, as part of the Serbian attempt to carve a corridor between Bosanska Krajina and Eastern Herzegovina that would encircle the Bosnian heartland and cut it off from Croat forces in Western Herzegovina.[82] The latter plan, however, was foiled by determined Croat resistance. Despite an agreement between the Bosnian Serb and Croat separatists on 6 May at Graz in Austria, failure to agree on the possession of Mostar led to a Croatian Army offensive that pushed Serb forces back from the Herzegovinian capital on 12–17 June. The Bosnian government's supply lines to the coast would remain open – so long as Croatia remained friendly. But the greater part of East Bosnia was conquered in April; the Užice Corps, in conjunction with TO forces from Užice (in Serbia) and the Chetniks and White Eagles, took Višegrad on the 13th. The 14,000 or so JNA troops who were officially not natives of Bosnia-Herzegovina were withdrawn from the country between 4 and 20 May. Subsequently Serbia's economic collapse, President Milošević's purge and downgrading of the JNA officer corps, international pressure and sanctions, widespread resistance to conscription, and political conflict between the Pale and Belgrade regimes, all impaired and eventually ended Serbia's ability to prop up militarily the Bosnian Serb parastate.

The system of 'general people's defence and social-self protection', which possessed its own staffs and units from 1976 until 1982 and through which the entire Yugoslav population was to be drawn into the defence of the country, was based upon a set of tactics many of which were employed to brutal effect by the SDS and the VRS in the 1990s. These included the responsibility of local political bodies to encourage 'the economic development of mountainous and frontier regions' as a future base of resistance;[83] to 'prevent the aggressor from employing the existing economic and service capabilities or exploiting the country's natural resources', by 'wrecking and rendering useless specific units of production' on the 'temporarily occupied territory'; to make preparations for the 'secret distribution of produced goods and their dispersal on the terrain, in secret warehouses', coupled with the 'complete destruction of production in warehouses employed by the enemy';[84] and most importantly 'to inform the working people and citizens of important questions of general people's defence and social self-protection … to motivate the population to an active involvement in defensive and protective activities', and 'to demonstrate in good time the sources and forms of threats to the freedom, independence and territorial unity and constitutionally determined social order [of the Yugoslav federation]'.[85] In the 1990s, the SDS would modify this system so as to mobilise the TO and the citizenry in Serb-majority areas, in order to kill and expel Muslims and Croats, destroy Bosnian cities and wreck the Bosnian economy. A similar case of inversion was the Serbian plan for the siege of Sarajevo, which according to Rasim Delić was a JNA plan for the *defence* of Sarajevo that had been drawn up immediately after World War II but was now adapted for the opposite purpose.[86]

The weaknesses in the Serbian strategy were first revealed by the JNA's failed attack on Sarajevo on 2–3 May. On the 2nd the JNA was prevented from plundering the Office of the Army in Sarajevo by the Green Berets and the citizenry, though Izetbegović's deputy Ejup Ganić had instructed the Staff commander of the TO in the Stari Grad not to oppose the plunder, for fear of jeopardising the President's negotiating position during international talks at Lisbon. Kukanjac then ordered a general attack on Sarajevo, the capture of the Presidency Building and the bisection of the capital; but JNA columns were surrounded or destroyed and JNA garrisons blockaded by the city's defenders. Kukanjac's convoy advancing from his headquarters in Bistrik was itself captured. Halilović and Efendić had successfully directed a counterattack involving the disparate forces of the MUP, Green Berets, TO and others.[87] The JNA attack involved the bombardment of the TV relay station at Hum as well as Sarajevo's central post-office and telephone exchange, and was followed that same day by the kidnapping of Izetbegović at Sarajevo airport as he returned from Lisbon, and by a coup attempted by Belgrade's Muslim agents in the Bosnian government, Abdić and Delimustafić.[88] This was the last, feeble attempt by Belgrade to conquer Bosnia-Herzegovina politically. It also involved the most serious split to date between Izetbegović and Halilović. The President had on 3 May agreed to allow Kukanjac's trapped column of 400 troops to evacuate the Bistrik barracks with their weapons and equipment in return for his release from JNA captivity, overriding objections from his fellow Presidency members; but Halilović had attacked the convoy anyway once Izetbegović was in Bosnian hands.[89] The Bosnian forces succeeded in capturing about a hundred JNA soldiers and thirty officers. Efendić subsequently wrote bitterly that a still greater victory and the capture of the entire convoy had been prevented by the intervention of the representatives of the UN and EU under General Lewis Mackenzie, who at all times worked to halt the Bosnian military actions and permit Kukanjac and his column to escape: 'We were naive beyond all measure. We trusted in the representatives of the European Union; we believed that they had been sent to help us, but they did everything to keep us in a concentration camp.'[90] Delimustafić was soon afterwards replaced as Interior Minister and the MUP brought under full government control, though it continued to conflict with the Army under Halilović. The unsuccessful 2 May offensive nevertheless gave Pale possession of sections of the capital, most importantly the relatively central ward of Grbavica where the homes of JNA officers and their families had been concentrated before the war.

The front lines in and around the capital would register only modest changes after early May. On the 13th negotiations over the JNA's withdrawal from Sarajevo broke down on the Bosnian insistence that it surrender the confiscated TO weapons.[91] On 16 May the JNA outside the city responded by attacking Pofalići, with the aim of capturing Hum, linking up with the besieged Marshal Tito Barracks and cutting the city in half along the line Pofalići-Vraca. Once again the JNA was repelled.[92] This offensive may have been coordinated with the JNA attack on Tuzla the previous day, in which it suffered a crushing defeat at the hands of the city's highly effective defence force grouped behind Bešlagić's Municipal Council Crisis Staff. As in Sarajevo two weeks earlier, the battle for Tuzla began with an attempt by the defenders to prevent the JNA removing confiscated TO weaponry from warehouses. JNA commander Mile Dubajić attempted to withdraw his troops from the JNA's Husino Uprising Barracks and link them with Serb forces attacking from Majevica, but his column was surrounded and largely destroyed in the Battle of Brčanska Malta.[93] A further attempt by Serb forces to cut Sarajevo in half was halted by the successful Bosnian defence of Žuč hill on 8 June and the liberation of Orlić, the highest peak in the hills north of the city.[94] Sarajevo could not be occupied or bisected and the besiegers lacked the manpower to conquer it in street fighting from without, as they had conquered the Croatian city of Vukovar. The Sarajevo-Romanija Corps of the VRS, which held Sarajevo in siege, numbered only about 28,900 troops during 1992; insufficient to conquer a city of well over half a million civilians and 35,400 defending troops.[95] The Serb conquest of the western city wards of Azići, Otes and part of Stup with heavy losses in December 1992 brought a successful Bosnian counteroffensive and advance at Žuč. Unable to take the capital, the Pale regime could only attempt to starve and bombard its civilian population, and with it the Bosnian government, into submission. This strategy was ultimately successful despite enormous cost to Pale's international image: the war ended in 1995 with a territorial settlement highly favourable to the Serb nationalists, due in part to the exhaustion of Sarajevo's citizenry and its desire for peace at almost any price, but Karadžić and Mladić paid for this success by their indictment as war criminals by the International Criminal Tribunal for the former Yugoslavia (ICTY). In the meantime, however, the military balance in the Sarajevo theatre would slowly shift in favour of the city's defenders.

While the VRS was unable to conquer Sarajevo, the ARBiH was equally incapable of breaking the siege. Throughout the war the ARBiH remained greatly inferior to the VRS in terms of heavy weapons. To a large degree, however, it was the political disunity of the Bosnian side that prevented the capital's defenders from breaking out, as much as Serb sectarianism prevented the besiegers from breaking in. According to Halilović and Alibabić, successful military operations from within the city against Serb positions at Vraca, Grbavica and Ilidža were halted by treasonous members of the government: Delimustafić, Abdić, Doko and Muslimović.[96] From 2–3 May repeated attempts by Bosnian forces at Visoko to breach the Serb ring from without failed, largely due to obstruction from the HVO stronghold of Kiseljak, which refused the TO passage through its territory.[97] The Kiseljak HVO enjoyed a warm relationship with the Serb besiegers, via whom they fed and milked the thriving black-market in Sarajevo at the expense of the citizenry. Criminal elements within the ARBiH too may have collaborated in maintaining the siege so as to profit from the resulting black market.[98] According to Hajrulahović there were no front lines or barricades at Igman because the frontier was in the hands of the mafia of all nationalities.[99] On Igman, too, there was conflict between the autonomous commanders who initiated the resistance and former JNA officers who arrived from Sarajevo and attempted to take charge of defences.[100] Jusuf Juka Prazina was a member of the local defence forces organised under the PL's umbrella in Sarajevo, who in the early months of the war had raised 3,000 troops to defend the capital. He became a folk hero and was appointed by Delimustafić commander of reserves in the MUP Special Forces. On the Igman front, he was by October 1992 guilty of indiscipline and repeated physical attacks on other Bosnian officers and officials. In November or December 1992 his men beat up representatives of the General Staff sent to coordinate Bosnian forces on the Igman front. One of Prazina's commanders claims that this occurred after a failure in communication during a coordinated offensive had resulted in the deaths of twelve of Prazina's men. Following this incident Prazina transferred his units to the command of the HVO, in keeping with the latter's plans for a Croat parastate extending through Kiseljak to include Igman and, possibly, part of Sarajevo. Prazina's forces were consequently disbanded by the Army in January 1993 in an engagement that cost two lives, and Prazina would subsequently fight on the side of the HVO against the ARBiH in Mostar.[101] The various criminals appear, however, to have enjoyed the protection of Halilović and of Izetbegović himself. Thus Halilović refused to contemplate the dismissal of Prazina in July 1992; Hajrulahović claimed Prazina was under Halilović's direct control.[102] Izetbegović maintained a close relationship with the Sarajevan gangster and ARBiH officer Mušan Topalović-Caco, allowing him to remain commander of the 10th Mountain Brigade so long as he did not threaten the President's own authority.[103] The ARBiH's defences on Igman would collapse in the summer of 1993 due to the corruption and treason of the local commanders.[104]

The ARBiH was a popular army that emerged overnight from a multiplicity of different local armed forces, each governed by a different combination of political elements. Such an army lacked the discipline of a professional army or one of long standing, and was prone to abuse by self-willed elements at the local level. One form that this abuse took was the formation of prison or concentration camps in which 'enemy' civilians were imprisoned and frequently killed or tortured. In May 1992 units of the ARBiH captured a number of Serb villages in the Konjic municipality in northern Herzegovina, killed or expelled their inhabitants and set up a prison camp at the village of Ćelebići. There Serb civilian prisoners were killed, tortured, beaten and sexually assaulted over a period of several months.[105] At the town of Visoko near Sarajevo a prison camp was set up for Serb prisoners of war in the spring or summer of 1992 at which the inmates were regularly beaten and forced to perform slave labour, such as the digging of trenches for the ARBiH.[106] Greater in scale were the war crimes carried out by forces under the command of Naser Orić, Commander of the Srebrenica Territorial Defence, which are alleged to have burned down at least fifty Serb villages and hamlets in the municipalities of Bratunac, Srebrenica and Skelani during 1992 and 1993.[107] Serb civilians in these municipalities were deliberately targeted and killed with great cruelty and thousands were driven from their homes.[108] ARBiH war crimes were not on the scale of those carried out by the VRS or HVO, however; nor is there any evidence that they were the product of a systematic policy of persecution of Serbs on the part of the Bosnian political and military leaderships. Bosnian Presidency member Mirko Pejanović, an ethnic Serb who intervened to secure the release of Serb civilians held in military prisons in Sarajevo, recalls that Sefer Halilović made a determined effort to stamp out such abuses, which led by late 1992 and early 1993 to the formation of a functioning system of military police and military courts and the gradual closing of the prisons.[109] But it was not until the autumn of 1993 that the criminal elements within the ARBiH guilty of terrorising Serb civilians in Sarajevo were finally suppressed, while 1993 also witnessed numerous war crimes against Croat civilians in Central Bosnia. Nevertheless, testimony to the ARBiH's success in this regard is the fact that its final, victorious offensive of 1995 was marked by a relatively benign treatment of Serb civilians; symbolic of this is the fact that in Donji Vakuf, taken from the VRS in September 1995, the town centre is still dominated by the Serb Orthodox church, while Orthodox and Catholic churches were untouched in Sarajevo, Tuzla and other ARBiH-held towns throughout the war. This is in stark contrast to the systematic destruction of mosques and Catholic churches in Banja Luka, Foča, Trebinje, Kupres and other towns held by the VRS. Orić himself was indicted by the ICTY and arrested as a war criminal in 2003.

Reorganisation of the Bosnian Army

The summer of 1992 marked a brief period of revival in Bosnian military fortunes prior to the catastrophes of the autumn, during which the organisation of the Bosnian armed forces and military effort assumed a more definite form. On 20 May 1992 the Staff of the TO of the Republic of Bosnia-Herzegovina was transformed into the 'General Staff of the Armed Forces of the Republic of Bosnia-Herzegovina', which provided the occasion for the replacement of Efendić by Halilović as commander on the 25th. Efendić attributes this to his having a Serb wife then resident in Belgrade and to the hostility of Doko, Halilović and the Croatian-oriented faction among the Bosnian leadership. Halilović likewise attributes his promotion to the support of the Croat members of the Bosnian government, Presidency member Stjepan Kljuić and Defence Minister Doko, who mistakenly believed that as a former JNA officer who had been stationed in Croatia he would be amenable to Croatian influence. Formally speaking, Halilović did not replace Efendić; rather, the latter's post of commander was formally abolished when the Staff of the Republic was abolished in favour of the General Staff of the Armed Forces.[110] Halilović's title was 'Chief of Staff', a factor that as we shall see would play a role in Halilović's own demotion the following year. Efendić was soon afterward appointed military attaché in Zagreb, something that he attributes to Halilović's wish to have him as far removed from the front as possible, as a witness to the latter's military incompetence.[111] On 22 May the TO Staff finally ordered the general mobilisation of TO forces throughout the Republic of Bosnia-Herzegovina, on the basis of the Presidency's 8 April declaration of a state of war-danger. On 27 May the formation of twelve TO brigades was announced by the Presidency. Several of these had in fact been formed earlier: the 1st Tuzla Brigade on 16 May; the 1st Zenica Brigade on the 18th; and the 2nd Tuzla Brigade on the 22nd. Other brigades formed or formally recognised that day were the 1st Podrina; the 1st Lukavac; the 108th Brčko; the 1st Bihaćka Krajina; four Sarajevo brigades; and the 'King Tomislav' under the command of the Croat Mate Sarlija Dajdža. No brigades were formed in Bosanska Krajina

(Western Bosnia) outside of the Bihać area. Of thirty new unit commanders appointed only two were non-Muslims.[112]

The newly recruited Rasim Delić was sent out of Sarajevo on 16 April to Visoko, a small town on the outskirts of Sarajevo, to form new units of the TO and to link them with the HVO units in the region, which were already acting in an increasingly autonomous manner. In Visoko, with the direct assistance of Hasan Čengić, Delić assembled a group of officers to assist in this process. On 3 June an Operational Command was established at Visoko under Delić's leadership to help organise and coordinate the formation of military units in the wider Sarajevo region. One of its tasks was to act as the funnel through which military supplies accumulated by Čengić from abroad would reach ARBiH units in Sarajevo and the surrounding area. Delić's Operational Command at Visoko would form a virtually autonomous system of command to which Izetbegović would give orders directly, bypassing the General Staff and Halilović in a manner the latter complained of as a violation of military protocol. However, the objective difficulties posed by the Staff of the Supreme Command in Sarajevo exercising jurisdiction over the Operational Command in Visoko when they were separated by Serb front lines led in autumn 1992 to the Operational Command being promoted into the 'Staff of the Supreme Command – Visoko Department', a further structural division of Army unity.[113] The 'Visoko group' of officers under Delić would provide the cadre for Izetbegović's reorganisation of the General Staff and demotion of Halilović a year later.

The Presidency finally declared a state of war and general mobilisation on 20 June 1992. A Presidential decree of 4 July on the reorganisation of the OS RBiH renamed the TO the Army of the Republic of Bosnia-Herzegovina. The ARBiH was to have a General Staff, okrug- and municipal-level staffs and to consist of corps, divisions, brigades, regiments, battalions, detachments, companies, squadrons and platoons. Stjepan Šiber, a Croat, played the leading role within the General Staff in devising a system of military salutes, manners, symbols and prefixes for unit names.[114] The OS RBiH was now to consist of two armies: the ARBiH and HVO, with a joint command. On 12 July 1992 Halilović secured Izetbegović's approval for the transferral of the General Staff from the jurisdiction of the Ministry of Defence to the direct jurisdiction of the Presidency, in order to bypass obstruction by the Croatian-oriented defence minister Doko.[115] The functional seat of the General Staff was in the autumn of 1992 established at Zenica, the city located at the geographical centre of Bosnia-Herzegovina. On 3 September the Presidency decreed the formation of five corps for the ARBiH: the 1st Sarajevo, 2nd Tuzla, 3rd Banja Luka, 4th Mostar and 5th Bihać, with the seat of the 3rd Corps to be located 'temporarily' at Zenica. These were based on the existing TO formations; thus the Okrug TO for Sarajevo become the 1st Sarajevo Corps of the ARBiH. Regional influence was important in determining the new corps commanders. Tuzla's proposal of the Croat Željko Knez for 2nd Corps commander was readily accepted by the Presidency, but a clash occurred over the post of 5th Corps commander. Irfan Ljubijankić, president of the Bihać Municipal Council, appealed to Izetbegović for the post to be given to the incumbent local commander Ramiz Dreković rather than to the General Staff's candidate. Halilović initially resisted, but after sending PL officer Rifat Bilajac to Bihać to check Dreković's credentials he accepted his appointment.[116]

Meanwhile, as the Bosnian state began its painful process of recovery and reorganisation, non-Muslim officials continued to peel off it much as non-Serb officers were peeling off the JNA. In March 1992 the Croat Branko Kvesić, deputy head of the SDB, fled to Mostar with several important documents to become deputy minister of police in the HZ H-B.[117] On 8 July Nenad Kecmanović, one of the two Serb members of the Bosnian Presidency, arrived in Belgrade and would subsequently denounce the Bosnian government and endorse the three-way partition of Bosnia-Herzegovina.[118] Kecmanović was helping to undo the work of his grandfather Vojislav Kecmanović, who had presided over the establishment of Bosnia-Herzegovina as a multi-national Republic of Serbs, Croats and Muslims in 1943–44. Other high-ranking defectors to the Serb rebels included Vitomir Žepinić, assistant Minister of Internal Affairs under Delimustafić. HDZ members among the Bosnian leadership attempted on 9 April 1992 to recruit the Croat Chief of Staff of the ARBiH Stjepan Šiber to be their 'representative' in the army command, who would then presumably have been expected to defect at the appropriate moment in the Bosnian Croat rebellion, but Šiber refused.[119]

THREE

Politicisation of the Bosnian Army, 1992–1994

The Bosnian Croat Rebellion

Bosnian recovery was dealt a crushing blow by the growing rebellion of the Bosnian Croat separatists under the guidance of Franjo Tuđman's regime in Zagreb. The 6 May 1992 agreement at Graz in Austria between the Bosnian Serb and Croat separatist leaders had delineated the borders of their prospective entities and accelerated the polarisation of Bosnian Croat politics, and on the 8th the HVO General Staff declared the HVO to be the only legal armed force on the territory of the HZ H-B. Consequently, two days later the Busovača Municipal Staff of the HVO repudiated its agreement with the Bosnian TO over the division of weapons, and gave the latter an ultimatum to surrender its weapons and put itself under HVO command.[1] In this way began the separation of the TO and the HVO – officially both components of the OS RBiH – that would lead to full-scale war between the two. Croatian President Tuđman's determined attempts to avoid conflict and to reach a compromise with Belgrade and the JNA (via the projected partition of Bosnia-Herzegovina agreed at Karađorđevo in March 1991) were the actions of a former Yugoslav Communist general who had spent the best part of twenty years in Belgrade collaborating with Serb Communists and generals. Similarly, the Bosnian Croat leaders of the HZ H-B centred on Western Herzegovina were mainly high functionaries from the defunct Communist regime.[2] Their collaboration with their SDS counterparts had often begun with common membership of the former Bosnian Communist Party, or had been arranged under the auspices of KOS.[3] Branko Kvesić, for example, had been an investigating judge in Mostar notable for his persecution of people singing Ustasha songs.[4] Just as Muslim JNA officers defected to the ARBiH, Bosnian Croat JNA officers defected to the HVO. According to Halilović, HVO Chief of Staff Milivoj Petković had been a JNA lieutenant colonel based in the Croatian town of Zadar under the future VRS commander Ratko Mladić, and had participated as commander of an artillery division in the JNA's bombardment of Zadar in 1991.[5] A report by the OSCE in Mostar, however, states that Petković had prior to the war been subordinate to Momčilo Perišić, Yugoslav Army Chief of Staff under Milosević.[6] Similarly, Ivica Rajić had remained in the JNA during its war against Croatia and offensive against East Bosnia, but in August 1992 defected to become HVO commander in Kiseljak, despite being suspected in Zagreb as a KOS agent. Rajić had till the time of his defection been engaged in intelligence-gathering activities on behalf of the JNA at the radar centre on Jahorina, directly south-east of Sarajevo. As warlord of Kiseljak, his smuggling of oil to the 'Serb Republic' and escalation of the conflict with the ARBiH meant that his defection scarcely marked a change of sides.[7] Rajić's defection coincided with the start of open conflict between the HVO and ARBiH in Kiseljak; on 5 August 1992 the Kiseljak HVO moved against the ARBiH, in order to prevent its consolidation, by seizing the main Kiseljak police-station as a prelude to its total occupation of the town.[8] Rajić would subsequently be indicted for war crimes by the ICTY for his role in the massacre of Muslim civilians at Stupni Do in October 1993.

The growing collaboration between the HZ H-B and the 'Serb Republic' led to the destruction by the HVO of HOS, a Croat militia opposed to collaboration with Serb forces. HOS was founded on 3 January 1992 in Ljubuški in Herzegovina and was the military wing of the Croatian Party of Right led by Dobroslav Paraga, which claimed that Bosnian Muslims were Islamicised Croats and which favoured the fusion of a united Bosnia-Herzegovina with Croatia. According to Halilović the HOS had immediately recognised the Bosnian President as its Commander-in-Chief and fought loyally on Bosnia-Herzegovina's behalf.[9] Unlike the HVO, the HOS accepted subordination to the Staff of the ARBiH, of which HOS commander Blaž Kraljević was appointed a member.[10] At a ceremony in the Herzegovinian town of Čapljina on 19 July 1992, at which both ARBiH and HOS representatives were present and at which the Bosnian and HOS flags were flown, Kraljević was reported as stating 'that HOS, as a regular army in Bosnia-Herzegovina, will fight for the freedom and sovereignty of Bosnia-Herzegovina because it is our homeland' and that it would 'not allow any divisions'.[11] Paraga later stated that HOS had been a constituent part of the OS RBiH and that Kraljević was the most senior OS RBiH commander in Western Herzegovina. He claimed that HOS's capture of the town of Trebinje in Eastern Herzegovina had violated the territorial demarcation between the 'Serb Republic' and HZ H-B agreed at Graz, in retribution for which the HVO assassinated Kraljević and his Staff on 9 August 1992 and forcibly incorporated the HOS into the HVO.[12] Just as the organs of the Bosnian state continued to persecute the PL even after the SDA's assumption of power, so the former Bosnian Communist officials at the head of the HDZ and HZ H-B suppressed the neo-Ustasha HOS. Opposition to the violent reordering of Bosnia-Herzegovina as a loose conglomerate of three politically and ethnically monolithic parastates would increasingly be confined to Bosnian-government territory, while the boundary between this territory and that of the HZ H-B became ever sharper.

Cooperation between the HVO and ARBiH broke down under the combined pressure of political disagreements, structural incompatibility and the treasonous politics of Croatian President Tuđman and his Bosnian Croat proxies, who favoured an agreement with the Pale Serbs at the expense of the Muslims. In October, the successful Croatian and Bosnian military operations against Serb forces in Bosanska Posavina, that had virtually severed the so-called 'northern corridor' linking Serb-occupied territory in western and eastern Bosnia, were dealt a stab in the back by Tuđman who had decided that Posavina should go to the Serbs.[13] The defence of the towns of Posavina had been hampered from the start by political conflicts over questions of Croat political separateness within Bosnia;[14] nevertheless, local Croats in Posavina had the will and ability to defend their native territory.[15] Officers of the Croatian Army who wanted to continue the struggle for Posavina found their movements crippled by Tuđman's agents within their own military and police, leading to the abandonment to Serb forces of the Bosnian town of Bosanski Brod, which fell on 8 October.[16] According to the dissident Croatian general Martin Špegelj, Bosanski Brod could have held out as strongly as Vukovar had it been earnestly defended.[17] Even HVO officers at Orašje east of Bosanski Brod blamed the fall of the latter on a political agreement at the highest state levels.[18] By contrast, when the central Bosnian town of Jajce fell on 29 October, ARBiH commander Zicro Suljević attributed the defeat to 'theoretical and political disagreements' between the HVO and ARBiH, that had prevented a convoy carrying ammunition and anti-tank weapons from reaching the besieged town.[19] Whatever the reasons for the fall of Bosanski Brod and Jajce, they represented catastrophic defeats for the ARBiH in terms of strategy and morale. The 2nd Corps of the ARBiH was forced to reign in its successful offensive in north-east Bosnia, that had liberated Kalesija and was due to liberate Zvornik, because of the new threat to its rear created by the fall of Bosanski Brod.[20]

Coincidentally or not, the fall of Jajce occurred only six days after the HVO's expulsion of the ARBiH and the Muslim population from the town of Prozor in Herzegovina on 23 October. Conflict broke out when the ARBiH raised the Bosnian flag in Prozor alongside that of the HZ H-B; the HVO responded by driving the former from the town.[21] In this way the clash between two rival state-building projects, Bosnian and Great Croatian, was sparked by the question of flags. Confidence in the imposition of one's own flag was a reflection of the possession of state power; the HZ H-B justified its attempt to impose its flag on Travnik with reference to the HVO's military contribution to the defence of the town.[22] Ante Prkačin, a former HVO commander critical of official HZ H-B policy, claims that while Muslim-Croat hostility in Central Bosnia originated with obstruction by the Muslims of early Croat actions against the JNA, the conflict escalated when it was made clear to the Muslims that Croat leaders wished to establish a Croat state. Particular resentment was aroused by attempts to make Muslims leaving Travnik sign a loyalty oath to the HZ H-B, and by the HVO's plundering of weapons and other goods destined for the ARBiH. By contrast, Muslim relations with the Posavina Croats was good because the latter did not engage in such acts of plunder.[23] Prkacin argues that the ARBiH ceased to tolerate HVO control of 30% of Bosnia-Herzegovina once it had become strong enough to put a stop to it.[24] Džemaludin Latić, former editor of the Bosnian newspaper *Ljiljan*, cites the HVO's plundering of humanitarian aid convoys as a major reason for the conflict.[25] The fundamental reason for the conflict, that two armies serving rival political projects were competing for control of the same strategically important territory, was given candidly in February 1993 by HVO Chief of Staff Milivoj Petković.[26]

Tuđman's anti-Bosnian policies brought to fruition the political and organisational conflicts inherent in the OS RBiH. As late as January 1993, Halilović was blaming the ARBiH-HVO conflict on Croat politicians, saying that without their interference he and Petković would reach agreement within minutes.[27] The final straw leading to all-out war between the ARBiH and HVO, however, was provided by the international community, whose 'Vance-Owen Peace Plan' (VOPP) of January 1993 divided Bosnia-Herzegovina into ten prospective provinces divided between Croats, Serbs and Muslims. This was taken by the Bosnian HDZ as legitimising its military possession of the three provinces assigned to the Croats. Bosnian Defence Minister and HDZ politician Božo Raić responded on 16 January by ordering all ARBiH units in the Croat provinces to submit to HVO command, and all HVO units in the Muslim provinces to ARBiH command, which resulted in fighting as the ARBiH resisted Raić's order.[28] Raić claimed that the conflict stemmed from elements in the ARBiH wanting to sabotage the VOPP and deny the Croats control of parts of the provinces assigned to them, and to Izetbegovic's refusal to put the ARBiH under HVO command in the Travnik and Mostar provinces.[29] In

April 1993, an HVO spokesman from Čapljina attributed the conflict with the Muslims to their refusal to recognize the Croat canton in Central Bosnia defined by the VOPP.[30]

The SDA leadership for its part responded to the VOPP by making preparations for the establishment of a Muslim state within Bosnia-Herzegovina, as a counterpart to the 'Serb Republic' and the HZ H-B. According to Musadik Borogovac, one of the Muslim participants in the negotiations over the VOPP, Izetbegović and Čengić responded to the Plan by drawing up the constitution of an 'Islamic state of Bosnia-Herzegovina', for whose establishment they were ready to make major territorial sacrifices, including turning over Mostar to the HVO.[31] By signing the VOPP, Izetbegović weakened the morale of the ARBiH and the readiness of its soldiers to fight for a unified Bosnia-Herzegovina, for soldiers were unwilling to fight for territories that had been surrendered politically.[32] Thus the signing of the peace plan encouraged partitionist sentiment within the ARBiH and helped prepare the ground for the establishment of a Muslim mini-state. In the event, the refusal of Karadžić's Serbs to sign the VOPP ensured that the SDA leadership was not able formally to establish a Muslim state at this time. Nevertheless the pro-partition policies of the Western powers undoubtedly encouraged both Bosnian Croat irredentism and Muslim separatism, which was quite likely their intention given their policy goals of partitioning Bosnia-Herzegovina and appeasing Serbia. It was perhaps not coincidental that on 3 January 1993 Bosnian Deputy Prime Minister Hakija Turajlić was murdered by Serb soldiers with the complicity of French UN forces. Turajlić was travelling from the UN-controlled Sarajevo airport into the city in a French UN convoy when it was stopped by VRS forces; the French UN commander opened the door of Turajlić's vehicle and permitted a Serb soldier to shoot him dead.

The HVO and ARBiH had begun as two interlinked military forces and their break was therefore messy, with individual commanders on both sides finding their loyalties pulled in two directions or able to intrigue with one side against the other. One example of this was ARBiH staff member Armin Pohara, a Muslim married to a Croat, who prior to the war had been president of the small, pro-Yugoslav 'Party of Mixed Marriages' based in Bosanski Brod, as well as the town's PL commander and vice-president of its Crisis Staff organised to resist the Serb threat. Pohara was early on dissatisfied by the Bosnian government's failure to react to the JNA shelling of Bosanski Brod in March 1992.[33] He was nevertheless promoted to the rank of general and to the ARBiH Staff by Izetbegović and continued to pursue an autonomous policy. Attached to the Tuzla-based 2nd Corps, Pohara joined the pro-Croat circle of 2nd Corps commander Željko Knez and, following the latter's dismissal in March 1993, was arrested for breach of military discipline.[34] According to Muhamed Borogovac, Pohara had acted as Izetbegović's agent in Tuzla and in that role had conspired against the Social Democratic mayor, Selim Bešlagić.[35] Be that as it may, Pohara remained a wild card. He was soon released and thereupon defected to the HVO, denouncing General Halilović as a traitor and accusing him of inciting the conflict between Muslims and Croats.[36] He thereupon founded the 'Muslim Democratic Party of Bosnia-Herzegovina', which took the side of Zagreb and the HVO against Sarajevo and the ARBiH. Along with Izmet Hadžiosmanović, former president of the Mostar SDA, and Fikret Abdić, former member of the Bosnian Presidency, Pohara thereupon became one of the prominent Muslim collaborators paraded by the Tuđman regime in its efforts to highlight the divisions in Muslim ranks before the international community.[37]

The Ideology at Birth of the Bosnian Army

The ARBiH was by January 1993 the only one of the three principal domestically recruited armed forces on Bosnian soil not to have embarked uncompromisingly on the road to ethnic homogeneity under the banner of nationalist extremism. Predominantly Muslim in composition, it nevertheless remained at least nominally dedicated to multi-national coexistence inclusive of all Bosnia-Herzegovina's peoples, and an unresolved tension existed between its all-Bosnian versus its more narrowly Muslim outlook. The oath taken by the Sarajevo PL ran as follows: 'I pledge to Allah that I shall defend the freedom and integrity of Bosnia-Herzegovina, my only homeland, whose borders are historical, lasting and indestructible, that I shall stand in defence of the peoples and citizens that are threatened, their religions, rights and freedoms. To that aim I am ready to sacrifice my life.'[38] While the pledge was directed to Allah, it promised defence of the land of Bosnia-Herzegovina, rather than the Bosniak or Muslim nation. Bosnian patriotism, rather than religious or ethnic identification, was the principal motivating force for Muslim officers of the ARBiH. Safet Zajko, commander of the 2nd Motorised Brigade of the 1st Corps, said in January 1993 that 'Death is difficult. But it is an honour to die for this, for Bosnia-Herzegovina'.[39] Rasim Imamović, commander of the 27th Krajina Brigade, said in October 1993 that he had joined the ARBiH in August 1992 in response to the aggression 'against my homeland Bosnia-Herzegovina'.[40] The ARBiH's ideological dilemma in 1992–93 was similar to that of the Partisans in 1941–42. The latter began as an overwhelmingly Serb force that in Bosnia-Herzegovina was recruited principally from Serb-peasant victims of the Ustashas. Following their split with the Chetniks, their Serb-nationalist rivals, the Partisans had nevertheless increasingly emphasised their defence of a multi-national Bosnia-Herzegovina and given priority to the recruitment of Muslims and Croats. The result was the establishment of a unified Bosnian Republic in 1943–45 under a multi-national government, albeit with a disproportionately Serb bureaucracy and armed forces. The position of the Bosnian Muslims in 1992–93 was in some sense analogous to that of the Bosnian Serbs in 1941–42 in that they were forced into armed resistance to an attempted genocide against them. That the ARBiH, unlike the Bosnian Partisans, was to evolve by the war's end in late 1995 into an almost wholly ethnically homogenous army in control of a rump Bosnian parastate dominated by a single nationality was not predetermined, but the result of the politics of the SDA regime.

Fikret Muslimović, who in the spring of April 1991 had served as Chief of Security in the Sarajevo Corps of the JNA, was to become the principal ideologue of the ARBiH as a Muslim army. His career is illustrative of the moral and ideological dilemmas facing JNA officers at the time of Bosnian independence. Muslimović writes how prior to the war his indignation as an orthodox Titoist was stirred by the attacks of Serb nationalists on the personality of Marshal Tito, the principle of brotherhood and unity and the legacy of the Partisans.[41] He argues that the Titoism of JNA officers who were not Serb nationalists led to complacency in the face of the dangers posed by the latter, who were not taken seriously as a threat to the unity of Yugoslavia.[42] This may account for Muslimović's own 180–degree ideological turnaround and his emergence as the SDA's favoured candidate for Commander of the ARBiH. His role prior to the outbreak of the war was itself highly ambiguous: as a military intelligence officer he belonged to KOS, one of the organs principally responsible for the planning of the Serb political and military campaign against Bosnia-Herzegovina, and may have vacillated between the JNA and Bosnian government or attempted to ride both horses for as long as possible. When in May 1991 a lorry containing arms arrived in Eastern Herzegovina from Serbia for delivery to SDS paramilitary forces, Muslimović claims he sent a team of intelligence officers to monitor the lorry and informed his superiors in Belgrade of the illegal action, as a result of which he was reprimanded for interference by KOS chief Vasiljević.[43] Alibabić and Halilović, however, claim that Muslimović prevented Bosnian security forces from apprehending the lorry and ensured that it remained safely in Serb hands. Alibabić claims further that the attempt by assistant Bosnian Minister for Police Avdo Hebib to block arms deliveries from Serbia to Serb rebels in Croatia led to his denunciation by Muslimović before the Sarajevo Military Court for interfering with JNA lorries.[44]

Muslimović for his part claims that following the elections in Bosnia-Herzegovina in later 1990 he did his best to facilitate talks between Izetbegović and the Yugoslav Defence Secretary General Veljko Kadijević, as a way of sidelining the SDS and preventing the JNA from falling wholly under Milošević's sway.[45] At all events, he defected to the Bosnian side on 15 April. At the end of April, according to Alibabić and Halilović, Delimustafić and Vasiljević attempted to have Muslimović installed at the head of the Bosnian State Security Service. Though this was vetoed by Alibabić, Muslimović acquired the post of Chief of Military Security in the

Republican Staff of the Bosnian TO.[46] When Halilović became Chief of Staff of the TO on 23 May, he sacked Muslimović from his post, but Izetbegović had him reinstated.[47] It was through the intervention of Muslimović, says Halilović, that another KOS officer, Enver Mujezinović, was at the end of May transferred directly from Belgrade to become a security official at the Bosnian Ministry of Defence, where he was protected by Doko.[48] Mujezinović would become Chief of the Bosnian State Security Service in May 1993. Muslimović and Mujezinović would play a decisive role in bringing about the replacement of Halilović as Commanding Officer of the ARBiH, an event of decisive importance for the future ideological orientation of the latter.[49] Yet set against Halilović's and Alibabić's accusations against Muslimović, Efendić claims that Muslimović in fact provided the ARBiH with vital military information: 'He developed an excellent intelligence network on the other side of the trenches and, thanks to him, we were extremely well informed, even of what was going on in the JNA General Staff and for that matter at Dedinje [the district of Belgrade where Milošević lived].'[50] Like Delimustafić, Muslimović may have been a double agent, collaborating with both sides so as to ensure his own survival regardless of which side won the war.

Halilović Sidelined

The replacement of Halilović had been considered by Izetbegović as early as July 1992. Šefko Hodžić, a journalist who has closely followed the politics of the ARBiH, attributes this to Halilović's military failures, to his failure to coordinate his actions with the Ministry of Defence and Ministry of the Interior, and perhaps to pressure from the HZ H-B, whose leaders were still formally in alliance with the Bosnian government and considered the Bosnian Chief of Staff their enemy.[51] According to Zulfikar Ališpago Zuka, subsequently deputy commander of the 6th Corps, Western 'support' for the desperate Bosnian government required an accommodation with Croatia and the halting of Halilović's successful offensive against the HVO, and consequently his dismissal.[52] This thesis is also supported by Mirko Pejanović, who records that Izetbegović wished to replace Halilović above all because he viewed him as a barrier to reconciliation with Zagreb and the HVO.[53] Halilović's book *Lukava Strategija*, however, attributes his own fall to his long-running conflict over policy and cadres with influential figures in the government, especially Čengić and Izetbegović himself. For example, in the spring of 1993 Izetbegović reprimanded Halilović for his resistance to demilitarisation of the East Bosnian enclaves of Srebrenica and Žepa in line with UN demands.[54] 'He constantly spoke of an end to the war, and I of a struggle for freedom' says Halilović of his disagreements with the President.[55] Muslimović was the SDA's favoured candidate to replace Halilović, while the Croats favoured former Croatian Army officer Jasmin Jaganjac. However, the successful Bosnian counter-offensive against Serb forces at Žuč in December 1992 temporarily rescued Halilović's reputation and his job.

The ARBiH nevertheless remained hampered by the policy of the Izetbegović regime, which combined a poor concept of military strategy with a desire to subordinate the army to its political goals, consequently the sidelining or dismissal of commanders who did not follow the SDA line. In the first four months of 1993, plans for the defence and liberation of the country and for breaking the siege of Sarajevo drawn up by Divjak, Šiber and other members of the General Staff were not even considered by the Presidency. Divjak would later talk of the marginalisation in this period of the first generation of Bosnian commanders in favour of less experienced newcomers.[56] In April 1993 Chief of Military Police Kerim Lučarević was sacked; he attributed his dismissal to his advocacy of a war of liberation, which he claims incited the hostility of Alispahić, Muslimović, Mujezinović, and others.[57] Finally, as the conflict between the ARBiH and HVO escalated, Croatian pressure for Halilović's replacement increased. The ARBiH suffered further military defeats in the spring of 1993, when Serb forces took the East Bosnian enclaves of Cerska and Kamenica, cut Goražde's lifeline, and brought Srebrenica and Žepa to the verge of collapse, while a Bosnian counteroffensive from within Sarajevo against Mt Trebević on 30 May was repulsed with heavy losses. These defeats provided the occasion for a change of commanders and a reshuffling of military cadres.[58] According to Izetbegović, an additional motive for demoting Halilović was a letter he received from Deputy Commander Jovan Divjak on 27 May complaining of the lawless behaviour in Sarajevo of the 10th Mountain and 9th Motorised Brigades, under the command of Mušan Topalović Caco and Ramiz Delalić Ćelo respectively. These units were terrorising Sarajevo's citizenry, above all ethnic Serbs, and were wholly resistant to the authority of the ARBiH Staff. Izetbegović implies that this required a shake-up of command cadres in the ARBiH to restore discipline.[59]

Izetbegović claims in his memoirs that the Bosnian Presidency initially offered the most senior post in the ARBiH in place of Halilović to the Partisan veteran and retired JNA general Džemil Šarac, but that the latter declined it. The post was then offered to Rasim Delić who accepted it.[60] Izetbegović presented to the Presidency his proposed reorganisation of the military high command on 2 June 1993. Halilović was formally to retain the post of Chief of Staff, but a new and senior post of Commander was to be created to which Delić would be appointed, with Jovan Divjak and Stjepan Šiber as deputies. Halilović, Delić, Divjak, Šiber and Muslimović were to be awarded the rank of General, while the five Corps commanders received the rank of colonel. Rifat Bilajac and Zicro Suljević, both founding members of the PL, were to be retired. A 6th Corps of the ARBiH was to be established, centred on Konjic and under the command of Salko Gušić. The Minister of Internal Affairs Jusuf Pušina, with whom Halilović had conflicted, was also sacked and replaced by Bakir Alispahić. Alispahić would take over direction of 'Ševa' ('Lark'), the secret police organisation that had been set up at the start of the war by Delimustafić and which included Muslimović and Mujezinović.[61] Alibabić became Chief of the Centre of the Security Service (i.e. chief of public and secret police), while Mujezinović replaced him as chief of the State Security Service (i.e. chief of secret police). Delić was recalled from duty in Tuzla to be told of his appointment on 5 June, while Halilović was informed two days later.[62] The following day, 8 June, a meeting of the Staff of the High Command was convened at which Halilović denounced the changes, in particular the promotions of

Delić and Muslimović, and threatened to resign.[63] Several founding members of the PL appear to have been violently opposed to the changes and to the fact that they had been enacted without consultation of the Staff: Bilajac, one of those retired, lamented that 'The Patriotic League has been defeated. The enemy has succeeded in turning one against the other';[64] Karavelić described the changes as 'a direct blow to the Patriotic League'.[65] Muslimović would later accuse Halilović of having attempted to incite the Staff of the High Command to a *coup d'état*. The officers of the Staff did indeed appear to be on the verge of rejecting the changes; according to Delić, it was Muslimović's plea – 'Before us is the order of the Supreme Command [i.e. the Presidency]. Do not permit the High Command to be obstructed' – that swung the assembly to acceptance of the changes.[66] Halilović would himself claim that his demotion had been unconstitutional since it had not been approved by the requisite majority in the Presidency.[67]

The changes of June 1993 represented an advancement for the 'Visoko group' of officers headed by Rasim Delić at the expense of the 'Sarajevo group' under Halilović. Several of Delić's subordinates from Visoko were promoted to leading positions in the General Staff in the capital, while Halilović's subordinates were marginalised.[68] Under the former PL-commander Halilović, a hawkish proponent of an uncompromising struggle for the military liberation of Bosnia-Herzegovina, the ARBiH had been an autonomous body whose policies and actions were pursued independently of the President and organs of government and whose functioning owed much to the Chief of Staff's personal control over the irregular forces in and around Sarajevo. Under Rasim Delić it would become a compliant tool of the President, wholly subordinate to the Izetbegović regime's political goals and dependent in turn on the President's personal control over irregular units.

Escalation of the War with the HVO

Events on the international plane would provide a further impetus for the Muslimisation of the ARBiH in the years that followed. The war with the HVO had escalated since the publication of the VOPP in January 1993, and to the surprise of the outside world it turned in the ARBiH's favour. The two armies had existed side by side in towns throughout Bosnia-Herzegovina, and the attempts by the HZ H-B leadership to establish a geographically cohesive 'state' territory left many HVO units in strategically unviable positions. The HVO was driven from Jablanica and Konjic in the spring of 1993; from Travnik and Kakanj in June; from Bugojno in July; and from Vareš in November. The HVO meanwhile was unable to dislodge the ARBiH from the eastern part of the Herzegovinian capital of Mostar: all-out war broke out there in May 1993 and, despite the gratuitous destruction of the town by the HVO and the regular Croatian Army, the front lines had barely shifted by the time of the Washington Agreement a year later. During 1993 the portion of Bosnian territory under HVO control fell by half, from about 20% to 10%. The ARBiH's victorious campaign was accompanied by large-scale atrocities against Croat civilians in Central Bosnia. The HZ H-B leadership claimed in August 1993 that since April of the same year the ARBiH had expelled the entire Croat population from the cities of Konjic, Jablanica, Travnik, Kakanj, Fojnica and Bugojno; destroyed 187 Croat villages; and imprisoned about 4,500 Croats in concentration camps.[69] Operation 'Neretva '93', launched at the end of August 1993, aimed at the liberation of Gornji Vakuf, Prozor and West Mostar from the HVO. On 7–8 September Bosnian forces killed 35 Croat civilians at the village of Grabovica. On 14 September Bosnian forces killed 29 Croat civilians at the village of Uzdol.[70]

In this period the ARBiH began forcibly to incorporate HVO units into its own military structure: the Sarajevo HVO brigade was incorporated into the 1st Corps on 6 November, and the Tuzla 115th HVO brigade into the 2nd Corps in December 1993 or January 1994.[71] This policy was endorsed by a Presidency decree on 14 December that required HVO units to be transformed into units of the ARBiH. In some localities, however, as in the towns of Tešanj and Olovo, the HVO remained an autonomous military force allied to the ARBiH, in keeping with local Croat opinion – soldiers of the 110th Brigade of the HVO in Tešanj were apparently appalled at the collaboration by the 111th Brigade of the HVO in nearby Žepče with the Serb enemy.[72] The ARBiH was nevertheless unable to inflict a decisive defeat on the HVO, or to drive it from the enclaves of Žepče, Kiseljak and the Lašva valley, where airlifted supplies from Croatia, collaboration with Serb forces and the ARBiH's lack of heavy weapons enabled it to hold out. Furthermore, Serb forces took advantage of the fighting between the ARBiH and HVO and of the change in Bosnian commanders to make further conquests in July and August: Trnovo, Bjelašnica, Treskavica and Grebak and Rogoj on Igman, all of which tightened the nooses around Sarajevo and the East Bosnian enclave of Goražde.

The full-scale war between the HVO and the ARBiH, sparked by the VOPP, accelerated the transformation of the HZ H-B from its official role as a temporary organization for Croat self-defence into the specifically sectarian, anti-Muslim entity with pretensions to full statehood that many of its champions had covertly intended it to be. Until early 1993 a significant part of the HVO was made up of Muslims. Full-scale war led to Muslim HVO troops crossing over to the ARBiH or being disarmed by their Croat commanders.[73] This process would lead to the establishment of concentration camps for Muslims; to HVO massacres of Muslim civilians, most notoriously at Ahmići on 16 April 1993 and at Stupni Do on 23 October 1993; to the destruction of mosques, continuing even after the signing of the agreement to set up a Muslim-Croat Federation in March 1994; and most infamously to the destruction of the Old Bridge at Mostar, along with the gratuitous demolition of half the town that the HZ H-B had supposedly wanted as its own capital. The Bosnian HDZ leaders also accelerated their establishment of a separate Bosnian Croat parastate, proclaiming the HZ H-B to be the 'Croat Republic of Herzeg-Bosna' (HR H-B) on 28 August 1993. This came in response to another Western diplomatic initiative, the drawing up of the Owen-Stoltenberg Peace Plan, which sanctioned a three-way carve-up of Bosnia-Herzegovina into a Muslim, a Serb and a Croat statelet. The HDZ leadership in Grude worked to radicalise those local HDZ and HVO bodies that, throughout Bosnia-Herzegovina, were during 1993 still striving to maintain good relations with local Muslim communities and with the Bosnian authorities. Thus the transformation of the HVO into a sectarian, anti-Muslim force began at the top political level and filtered downwards. One example of how this transformation took place is that of Fojnica, a town in Central Bosnia where local Croats maintained good relations with Muslims during the first year of the war, forming a town government in which the two nationalities were represented in equal numbers. In June 1993 the HVO command dismissed Fojnica's Croat leadership following the refusal of the latter to mobilise the town's Croat militia in the war against the ARBiH. The HZ H-B leadership appointed a Croat from Herzegovina as the new leader of Fojnica's Croats and brought HVO forces from outside for a full-scale assault to drive the ARBiH from the town. When the ARBiH drove off the encircling HVO forces in an offensive beginning on 2 July, most of the town's Croat inhabitants also fled. In their counter-offensive to recapture Fonjica on 10 November, HVO forces burned down two mosques in the nearby village of Olavak.[74]

A more extreme case of the HZ H-B leadership's deliberate sabotaging of peaceful coexistence between the HVO and ARBiH at the local level is that of Vareš, an old industrial town with a politically moderate plurality Croat population. Following the elections of 1990 political power was shared in Vareš between the HDZ, the SDA and the Social Democrats, while military power was shared between the Muslim-led Territorial Defence and the locally formed HVO, all of which were committed to peaceful multi-national coexistence between Croats, Muslims and Serbs. This situation was unacceptable to Mate Boban's HDZ regime in Grude and on 28 June 1992 the Vareš HVO was ordered by its superiors to seize complete control over the town, which it proceeded to do three days later. This prompted the SDA's secession from the Vareš Municipal Council, but the local HVO authorities nevertheless strove to protect the lives and property of local Muslims and Serbs and continued to fly the Bosnian flag, alongside that of the HZ H-B, over the municipal assembly building. In June 1993 the town's multi-ethnic relations were poisoned by the arrival of several thousand Croat civilian and military refugees fleeing the town of Kakanj, which had just fallen to the ARBiH. The Kakanj Croats attacked local Muslims and those that were mobilised into the Vareš HVO, disregarding the local *modus vivendi* with the ARBiH. They continuously provoked the latter, attacking its positions and killing its soldiers. This behaviour was encouraged by Boban's HZ H-B leadership in Grude, which informed the exiled Kakanj Croat leadership of its displeasure with the Vareš HVO. Eventually, as the Kakanj soldiers' provocations drew an increasingly strong ARBiH response, the Vareš HVO appealed to the nearby HVO-held town of Kiseljak for support. Kiseljak was the fiefdom of the former KOS agent Ivica Rajić. On 21 October, Rajić's HVO special forces arrived from Kiseljak to carry out a coup against the moderate Vareš leadership. The new regime immediately began a reign of terror against local Muslims, massacring over 80 in an attack on the village of Stupni Do on 23 October. According to Vareš's moderate HDZ mayor Anto Pejčinović, this was a deliberate policy aimed at provoking an ARBiH occupation of the town that would enable the HR H-B leadership to resettle the Vareš Croats in areas of Herzegovina cleansed of Muslims: the HR H-B had already ceded Vareš diplomatically to the Muslims and had no interest in its survival under local, independent Croat leadership. Thus provoked, the ARBiH occupied Vareš on 4 November.[75]

Operation Trebević

The late summer and autumn of 1993 represented the lowest point in Bosnia-Herzegovina's fortunes, as its Serb and Croat enemies closed ranks and the Western powers and the UN moved to endorse its full partition. These factors encouraged a defeatist mood among the Bosnian leadership, among which voices were heard calling for the acceptance of partition and the establishment of a Muslim republic incorporating approximately one-third of the country. The commitment of Izetbegović and his circle to Bosnian unity continued to weaken; the President addressed the Bosnian parliament on 27 August 1993 to state that: 'In the meantime it appears that we must be partitioned. We can do this at the negotiating table, or on the battlefield in the war in which, unfortunately, all laws are gradually disappearing …'[76] According to Rusmir Mahmutćehajić, in this period Muslimović and others close to the President began propagating the idea of a change in war aims to encompass only those territories in which the Muslims had formed a majority prior to the war.[77] Adnan Jahić, a prominent member of the SDA from Tuzla, published a proposal on 17 September 1993 for a 'Virtuous Muslim state' based on 'the territory controlled by the Bosnian Army after the war', as the 'national state of Bosniaks, or Muslims', governed by a 'Muslim ideology, based on Islam, Islamic religious, legal, ethical and social principles, but also on the values of Western origin which do not contradict Islamic principles.' Jahić claimed that this project had the approval of Izetbegović himself.[78] On 27 September a special 'Bosniak assembly', convened in Sarajevo by Izetbegović and comprising prominent members of the Muslim political and cultural establishment, voted on whether to accept the Owen-Stoltenberg Plan, that would have effectively endorsed the partition of Bosnia-Herzegovina, the annexation of two-thirds of the country to a Great Serbia and a Great Croatia, and the formation of a Muslim national state from the remainder. The assembly's rejection of the Plan ended the possibility of formal establishment of a Muslim state; but the SDA leadership would continue to pursue the goal covertly, while remaining formally committed to a unified Bosnia-Herzegovina.

The second stage in the President's subordination of the ARBiH, following the sidelining of Halilović in June, would occur in late October 1993 with 'Operation Trebević'. This was a military operation by the Army and police against the 9th Motorised and 10th Mountain Brigades commanded by the Sarajevan gangsters Ramiz Delalić Ćelo and Mušan Topalović Caco, that controlled a large part of the besieged capital. Initially effective and obedient military leaders, Topalović and Delalić became increasingly self-willed and indisciplined during 1993 as Bosnian state power crumbled, and their units were gradually transformed into private armies in the service of their criminal fiefdoms. They paralysed the functioning of state and legal bodies in the capital and carried out a reign of terror against civilians, particularly Serbs and Croats.[79] Topalović and Delalić appear to have enjoyed a close relationship with Halilović. Hajrulahović, as commander of Sarajevo's defences, claimed subsequently that Halilović had exercised an informal system of authority over the gangsters, who had regarded him as their 'grandfather'.[80] The 9th and 10th Brigades were therefore feared as units in the service of Halilović's personal policies. On 2–3 July 1993, following the arrest of one of Topalović's underlings on Muslimović's order, these brigades had seized control of the police station in Sarajevo's Stari Grad and arrested and disarmed over two hundred policemen.[81] This occurred in the context of Halilović's power struggle with the Ministries of the Interior and Defence – Defence Minister Munib Bišić later accused Halilović of having at this time disarmed hundreds of policemen in the Stari Grad.[82] Izetbegović succeeded in negotiating the withdrawal of the rebel troops and their return to barracks, but immediately summoned Commander Delić and Interior Minister Alispahić to arrange the suppression of the 9th and 10th Brigades.[83] On 7 July Halilović's apartment was blown up in what may have been a failed attempt to assassinate him by the Ševa police organisation and which claimed the lives of his wife and brother-in-law.[84]

The Bosnian government launched Operation Trebević after months of careful planning on 26 October, masterminded by Mujezinović, the former KOS officer and head of the State Security Service. The military operation was immediately preceded by a request from the Executive Council of the SDA to 'undertake measures to reestablish order and respect for the law so as to restore the faith of the citizens in their army and state.'[85] The bloody showdown claimed seventeen lives and involved elite Army and police units in a force numbering about 3,000. Delalić was persuaded to surrender and arrested, but Topalović resisted and killed nine policemen before being captured, tortured and killed.[86] During the course of the action Halilović was blockaded in his office by the police.[87] 61 Bosnian soldiers of the two rogue brigades were subsequently charged with mutiny, while the remainder were distributed among loyal units of the ARBiH. The operation coincided with the final dismissal of Halilović as Chief of Staff and the start of an investigation into his alleged misconduct, in which he was accused of collaboration with Topalović and Delalić. The purge of Topalović and Delalić was followed on 6 November by the forcible incorporation of the HVO's 'King Tvrtko' Brigade in Sarajevo into the ARBiH's 1st Corps, with 1st Corps commander Vahid Karavelić claiming that the unit had collaborated with the Serb besiegers and that HVO membership had provided a cover for draft dodging in the besieged capital.[88] The presidium of the HDZ's Sarajevo branch responded by demanding that the Bosnian government halt its 'aggression' or it would request that the UN evacuate the Croat population from the capital.[89]

The Bosnian government was asserting control in its own backyard. While this meant a restoration of the rule of law and a stronger and more stable state, it also ensured the unhindered imposition of the SDA's political ideology on the ARBiH and eventually the complete abandonment of the latter's multi-national character. Operation Trebević was followed two days later by a reconstitution of the Bosnian government and the appointment of Haris Silajdžić as Prime Minister. The Bosnian government had up till then been a largely non-functioning institution, with key posts, such as the premiership and Ministry of Defence, in HDZ hands. In the new Bosnian government most of the key posts, including the premiership and the ministries of the Interior, Defence, Foreign Affairs, Finance, Justice and the Economy, were given to Muslims. The government would henceforth be subordinated increasingly to Izetbegović and the SDA. Another change was that Rusmir Mahmutćehajić, the once-powerful Minister of Energy and Industry, was demoted to Minister of Special Production; Izetbegović claimed later that he had been attempting to use his control over energy supplies to establish control over the Army.[90] Mahmutćehajić was finally dismissed from the government in January 1994.

Operation Trebević was followed by a series of purges of Army officers and state officials across the country over the course of the next year, beginning with the arrest of 180 people in Konjic, seat of the new 6th Corps of the ARBiH established with the demotion of Halilović. The sacked Konjic police chief attributed his fall to the hostility of former JNA officers to him as a founder of the Green Berets militia.[91] There was no military reason for the formation of the 6th Corps, according to its former Chief of Information Service, Murat Kahrović, who claims it merely created confusion among the military units in the region.[92] The 6th Corps was therefore probably formed for the political purpose of asserting the regime's control in the region to the south of Sarajevo, and was disbanded the following year after this goal had presumably been achieved. The regime's subordination of the Army to its political and diplomatic goals and its purge of independently minded commanders in the military and security forces, already marked, now accelerated. In January 1994 the War Council for the Supreme Command of Defence, the military advisory body formerly called the Military Council that had included senior members of the Presidency, parliament and government, including several non-Muslims, was reorganised so that its composition became predominantly military: it was now made up of the ARBiH corps commanders, while former civilian members such as Mirko Pejanović lost their places.[93] In January 1994 the legendary commander of the Special Forces of the Sarajevo MUP, Dragan Vikić, was shifted by Alispahić to a purely administrative post where he lost all influence over Sarajevo's defences.[94] In August 1994 Munir Alibabić, an opponent of Muslimović and Mujezinović, was sacked as the Republic's Chief of Police – a post he had held despite having been Chief Prosecutor in the 1983 show trial of the future SDA leadership.[95]

FOUR

The Bosnian Army Comes of Age, 1994–1995

The Shift to a Bosniak-Nationalist Ideology

The ideology of the ARBiH, as elaborated by General Muslimović, involved the complete identification of the Army with the SDA and the Muslim, or rather Bosniak, nation. Muslimović wrote in March 1994 that the successes of the liberation struggle were due to the 'high level of political organisation of the Bosniak nation, to which the SDA gave its principal meaning and stamp. Of particular service were the SDA and its cadres, and particularly the President of the Presidency of the Republic of Bosnia-Herzegovina Mr Alija Izetbegović ... The prestige of our Army is at once the prestige of our nation, and the prestige of our nation is inseparable from the prestige of the SDA.'[1] For Muslimović, all aspects of state were to be subsumed within the organisation and ideology of the ruling Party:

> *The SDA has accepted the historic responsibility to protect the nation and safeguard the state in which we shall be able to live in a normal manner. For the realisation of this goal our party, as a political factor, participates in the organisation of the state, the organisation of the Army of the RBiH, the MUP and all other institutions of state, which means that it in practice organises the whole of the liberation struggle ... As we have responsibility for the Army, which within the framework of our*

politics is the bearer of the armed struggle, so we have responsibility for radio, television, newspapers etc ...[2]

This advocacy of a Party army was coupled by Muslimović to the reaffirmation of Bosniak nationhood and Islam among the Bosnian Muslims: their ideological, religious and cultural homogenisation. In January 1995 the ARBiH Press Centre published a booklet entitled 'Moral Aspects of Defence', which had arisen from a seminar organised by the Office for Morale of the General Staff, in which Muslimović laid down his ideology of Bosniak national resistance. He claimed that the Serbian and Croatian plans for extermination of the Bosnian Muslims arose 'exclusively from the fact that they are Bosniak-Muslims and that the basis of their identity, their spirit, their customs and their traditions is Islam. They wish to nullify Islam, so that all traces of its existence in this region be lost.'[3] In reference perhaps to his own political and professional past, Muslimović argued further that the ground for genocide was prepared by the Muslims' forty-five-year experience of 'brotherhood and unity' within Titoist Yugoslavia, that denationalised them and robbed them of their political cohesion: 'separation from the important determinants of the identity of the Bosniak-Muslim nation, from their customs, their culture, their religion and their collective traditions, served the function of political disablement of the Bosniak-Muslims ...'[4] The solution followed naturally:

The goal of the liberation struggle for the Republic of Bosnia-Herzegovina is a unified, democratic state in which every citizen, every nation and every religion will have full freedom and one will not exclude another.

Taken alone, this statement would imply support for Bosnia-Herzegovina as a state of citizens rather than of Muslims. However, continued Muslimović:

That goal of the liberation struggle for the Bosniak-Muslims means to establish circumstances in which they can freely and unrestrainedly express and entrench themselves, in all their customary, cultural, religious and in all senses traditional particularity, in keeping with their political interests and everything that belongs to them, without damage to similarly registered interests of the Serbs and Croats. Since Islam is the most important foundation of Bosniak-Muslim particularity, this means that the Bosniak-Muslims must tell everybody that the goals of their liberation struggle necessarily and implicitly involve the survival of Islam in the Republic of Bosnia-Herzegovina; that Islam, like Catholicism and Orthodoxy, have unlimited freedom ... The Bosniak Muslims do not want an Islamic state. They want a normal state in which Islam will also be free.[5]

In other words, Muslimović articulated an integral Muslim nationalism, as a guiding force for a Bosniak — not Bosnian — liberation struggle, whose attitude to the Bosnian Serbs and Croats was not hegemonic but separatist: each of the three peoples would be free to affirm and enjoy its national particularity. The ARBiH would therefore cease to be a Bosnian Army and become a Bosniak Army. The contradiction inherent in a liberation struggle that on the one hand limited its political base to the Muslim nation, whose distinctiveness from the Serbs and Croats it aimed to enhance, and on the other was conducted under the banner of a united Bosnia-Herzegovina, would soon become readily apparent.

In the view of Halilović and Alibabić, as expressed in their published memoirs, Muslimović's espousal of a Muslim-national army represented the secret agenda of KOS, which by ending the multi-national character of the ARBiH ensured it would become not an obstacle but an accomplice to the partition of Bosnia-Herzegovina by Serb and Croat nationalists. Whatever his motives, Muslimović merely gave expression to the dominant trend in the SDA's view of the Army and the war. His influence within the ARBiH, though powerful, was not dominant. He appears to have attempted to obstruct the appointment of Delić as Commander in June 1993,[6] but was subsequently responsible for writing most of Delić's public statements and, according to one source, fifty percent of his written directives.[7] There was to be a major clash between the two men in the months following Dayton, when Delić vetoed suggestions that Muslimović be appointed head of military intelligence. The Army nevertheless increasingly adhered to the ideological model favoured by Muslimović. In 1994, the Staff of the High Command published a *Manual for the Squad Leader* that defined the purpose of training and education as being 'that soldiers and their superiors recognise and adopt the goals of the liberation struggle, the establishment and safeguarding of the Bosnian state, the worth of Bosniak tradition and culture, and, linked to that, the building of consciousness of the importance of the defence of the freedom and independence of the Bosniak nation.' Members of the ARBiH were further required 'to adopt and accept the Bosniak orientation of the liberation war, the worth of the Bosniak nation, the free profession of religion and custom'.[8] Furthermore,

> *The principle of Bosniak education, orientation and instruction expresses the demand that the entire process of training and education must be founded on the worth of Bosniak culture and tradition and, in particular, the worth of the concept of the liberation war, as well as on the basic standpoints and practical politics of the state leadership in questions of the defence of the country.*[9]

General Delić nevertheless continued to pay lip-service to the importance of the Army's multi-national composition, since 'Paramilitary formations cannot be related to the nations [sic.]. We do not want to have a nationally clean army [sic.]'.[10] This may have represented a sensitivity to international public opinion, but also an outlook that diverged from that of Muslimović and other proponents of a Muslim army. According to Delić in March 1994: 'I should say that the orientation and aim of the Army's activity is more important than its ethnic composition. And the aim is Bosnia-Herzegovina's statehood.'[11] Delić may have himself had problems with the 'peace negotiations' being conducted by the government, and in September 1993 he complained of soldiers being unwilling to fight for territories ceded to Serb or Croat entities by the diplomacy of the international community.[12]

The ARBiH was being transformed into a Bosniak/Muslim-national army, which implied neither complete ethnic homogeneity nor Islamic fundamentalism. The Army's Press Centre in February

1994 published a booklet entitled *The Spiritual Force of Defence*, which had arisen from a seminar on 'The role of religion in strengthening the patriotic unity of the defence and liberation forces' held the previous month in Sarajevo. Contributors to the seminar and booklet stressed the importance of Islam and the Islamic Community of Bosnia-Herzegovina in Army morale. Rašid Muminović, Chief of the Department of Religious Affairs at the Army's Office of Political Affairs, stated that 'the Islamic Community does not wish that it be concerned only with 'the needs of the believer', but that the science of Islam and the Muslim tradition be the basis for the morale of the Muslim-Bosniaks, particularly if we want the 'Army to resemble its nation' !'.[13] Muslimović himself argued for an enhancement of the Islamic Community's role in combatting anti-religious manifestations within the Army and called upon unit commanders to pay more attention to the role of religious counsellors within their units and to the performance of religious duties by their soldiers.[14] Nevertheless, Muslimović argued against any discrimination against non-Muslim soldiers or pressure on them to accept Islamic values.[15] The Reis-ul ulema of Bosnia-Herzegovina Mustafa Cerić, speaking at an ARBiH seminar in January 1994, stated: 'in this Bosnia, Allah the Almighty from one man and one woman created different peoples and different tribes, so that they might help and understand each other. Thus there is a land called Bosnia in which live different people, and that is the law enacted by Allah the Almighty.'[16] He proclaimed: 'This is a time when Allah commands us not to be concerned for Christians and Jews, but for the lives of Muslims, to care for their religion, to care for their freedom, for their possessions and their honour'; nevertheless, 'in Bosnia there will yet be the scent of different roses.'[17]

Rather than becoming an Islamic fundamentalist army committed to a religious struggle, the ARBiH was being transformed into a Bosniak-national army committed to a national-liberation struggle to which Islam was subordinated and for which it served as a badge. 'Islamic patriotism' or 'religious patriotism' were equated with the 'Bosniak liberation struggle'.[18] In July 1996 the General Staff published a collection of quotations from the Koran to provide comfort to war invalids.[19] However, some individual Army units did tend towards the standpoint that they were fighting a religious struggle. The commander of the 7th Muslim Brigade stated in June 1994: 'this unit was joined above all by men who carried with them a good domestic upbringing, Muslim patriotism and belief in Allah the Almighty. All those who did not wish to fight where Muslim sanctity was abused, who firmly believed that without belief in Allah there is not his mercy nor therefore victory, came to us'[20] and that 'the struggle for self-defence is an order from Allah the Almighty'.[21] The commander of the 37th Muslim Light Brigade stated in August 1994 that his unit was 'organised on Islamic principles'[22] and that 'I want to develop a high level of Islamic consciousness among my troops.'[23] An officer for moral guidance in the elite 'Black Swan' units, whose soldiers were required to abstain from drinking and swearing and to pray collectively on Friday, stated: 'Our religion is the foundation of our nation. In that way we and our culture differ from the Croats and Serbs !'.[24] Units such as the 7th Muslim Brigade and the Black Swans may have formed the basis for a parallel system of command exercised by Izetbegović and Čengić, which like Rasim Delić's 'Visoko group' bypassed the General Staff and thus acted as precursor to a wholly Party-based army.[25]

The Federation of Bosnia-Herzegovina

A decisive event for the subsequent history of Bosnia-Herzegovina and the ARBiH was the Washington Agreement of March 1994, arrived at under US auspices, that ended the war between the ARBiH and a mangled HVO that by then existed merely as a cover for operations by the regular Croatian Army. This represented a new US policy of bringing the war in Bosnia-Herzegovina to a close by altering the military balance at the Serb side's expense, so as to force it to the negotiating table. The Washington Agreement envisaged the establishment of a loose Bosnian 'Federation' that would encompass the territories under ARBiH and HVO control and supersede the existing state formations, the Republic of Bosnia-Herzegovina and the HR H-B. The Federation was to have a 'unified military command', yet in the transitional period leading up to its establishment 'current command structures will remain in place'.[26] The ARBiH and HVO were to be united in a Federation Army, but retain their separate structures. On 11 March 1994 the Split Agreement was signed between Generals Rasim Delić and Ante Roso, as commanders of the ARBiH and HVO respectively, as a preliminary to the establishment of a Joint Staff. This agreement was reached under the auspices of the USA's General John Galvin, and US military representatives would thenceforth invest considerable effort into attempting to forge the two armies into a functioning unified force.[27] The most immediate effect of the Agreement was to end any possibility of a Serb military victory. Bosnian troops redeployed from the front line with the HVO lifted the siege of the Central Bosnian town of Maglaj. Further Serb gains would be possible only at the expense of the besieged enclaves of East Bosnia such as Goražde, which came close to falling in April 1994, or Srebrenica and Žepa, which fell in July 1995.

While improving the ARBiH's military position, however, the Washington Agreement accelerated its transformation into a purely Muslim army. The Bosnian government and the Staff of the High Command were immediately forced to abandon their policy of incorporating the HVO into the ARBiH.[28] In the Tuzla area, for example, the 115th Brigade of the HVO had been incorporated into the 2nd Corps in the months immediately prior to the Agreement, but the 108th Brigade of the HVO was not, for fear of adding grist to the mill of the Croat nationalists.[29] In later months the threat of Croat-Muslim conflict in the Tuzla area was averted by Mayor Bešlagić visiting Croat villages around Tuzla and promising local Croats full security, though insisting that they play their part in the defence of the region. Tuzla Croats unwilling to join the ARBiH were to be permitted to join the HVO's 108th Brigade. The President and Vice-President of the Bosnian Federation, a HDZ and an SDA politician respectively, subsequently visited Tuzla to make the necessary arrangements.[30] In other words, the incorporation of the Tuzla HVO into the ARBiH was halted, and the division between the two armies reaffirmed, through the mediation of the nationally based parties at the head of the state. In December 1994 the newly appointed commander of the 2nd Corps, General Sead Delić, demanded the subordination of HVO forces in the Orašje enclave of north-east Bosnia to his command. This was rejected by the Ministry of Defence of the HR H-B as a violation of the Washington Agreement.[31] Furthermore, the establishment of a Federation under joint state institutions in which the HR H-B leaders would be guaranteed representation threatened a degree of Croatian influence over the Bosnian state and consequently of the Army. Over the course of 1994, therefore, the Staff of the High Command was renamed the General Staff, and all remaining functions related to the Army were removed from the jurisdiction of the Ministry of Defence and united under its aegis.[32] The General Staff appeared intent on remaining independent of the Presidency of the Federation; was accused by Croatian sources of obstructing the formation of a Joint Staff, even as it demanded a full merger of the HVO and the ARBiH into a unified military force.[33]

The ARBiH was becoming a party army of the SDA, independent of the formal state bodies. In December 1994 the 2nd Corps commander General Hazim Šadić, who had been under fire for his close relationship with the Social Democratic Mayor Bešlagić,[34] was replaced by Sead Delić, a supporter of the SDA. Sadić had championed the idea of a multi-national Army and in July 1994, in conjunction with representatives of Tuzla's loyal Serb community, had established a 'Serb Liberation Battalion' within the 2nd Corps as a political statement directed at the Serb population behind enemy lines.[35] This was a throwback to the policy of the Bosnian Partisans, who in 1943 had sought to recruit more Muslims and Croats to their predominantly Serb forces by establishing a Muslim and a Croat brigade; not coincidentally, it was also in Tuzla and the wider region of north-east Bosnia that this experiment was undertaken. Yet such a policy ran counter to that of the Izetbegović regime. Delić rejected the idea of extending the system of Serb military units in north-east Bosnia, for fear that it would damage the unity in command between the ARBiH and HVO in northern Bosnia by providing a pretext for the HVO command to extend its control over north-Bosnian HVO units at the expense of the 2nd Corps.[36] Furthermore, Sadić and Bešlagić may have been suspected by the Izetbegović regime of harbouring autonomist designs for the Tuzla region in collusion with the local HDZ and HVO;[37] and in October 1993 the commander of the 107th Brigade of the HVO in Gradačac in north-east Bosnia had been reported as calling for autonomy for the region.[38] By contrast, Sead Delić would state following his appointment: 'I recognise that the SDA was the party that organised this nation and succeeded in defending it. I think it is necessary that at this time we comprise a single party, which would strengthen our ranks.'[39] Sadić's project of forming Serb units was therefore discontinued by his successor.

The transformation of the ARBiH into the private army of the SDA meant in turn the ever greater personal control over it of Izetbegović himself. On 16 April 1994 Muslimović, as Deputy Chief of Staff, announced that the Army's Department for Morale would begin to celebrate the President's Cult of Personality:

At the Department for Morale, the Staff of the High Command of the Armed Forces of the RBiH is commencing an academic project entitled 'The personal role of Mr Alija Izetbegović in the defensive organisation of the nation'. One of the methods of this research will be to analyse the contents of statements, announcements and written documents of which the author is Mr Alija Izetbegović, as well as to analyse the contents of documents – decisions of the Presidency of RBiH, as well as positions and conclusions of the leadership of the SDA – in whose conception Mr Izetbegović played a key role.[40]

On 20 October 1994, at a ceremony at Zenica, Izetbegović was proclaimed 'honorary commander' of the 7th Muslim Brigade and received a certificate written in Bosnian and Arabic according to which:

We fighters of the 7th Muslim Illustrious Brigade, by the Lord Allah the Almighty in whose name we fight, proclaim our immense honour in awarding this certificate to the hadji Alija Izetbegović, the most worthy son of Bosnia, most beloved brother of the Bosniak-Muslim nation, proclaiming you first honorary commander of the 7th Muslim Illustrious Brigade. It is our principle: May the mercy of Allah, and His protection

*from the crime committed against the Bosniak-Muslim nation, always
be with you.*[41]

This ceremony provoked a clash between Izetbegović and his self-
appointed 'Vice-President' Ejup Ganić on the one hand and the
non-SDA members of the Bosnian Presidency on the other. The
latter, as one of the last feeble bastions of multi-national pluralism
in the state, on 30 January 1995 condemned the politicisation of the
ARBiH as expressed at Zenica and its transformation into an
Islamic, Bosniak and SDA army.[42] Izetbegović reacted with fury and
contempt directed at his fellow Presidency members, stating: 'The
7th Muslim has with its fighting objectively done more to safeguard
a Bosnia of citizens than all those self-proclaimed, vociferous
democrats who sit at home and just talk about Bosnia', and
promising that members of the ARBiH 'will not be persecuted for
their religion, nation or political beliefs.'[43] This was despite the fact
that members of the Presidency, which was still formally the
Supreme Command of the ARBiH, had every constitutional right to
make their voices heard with regard to the latter. Nevertheless, they
were publicly denounced by SDA elements in the media as
Communists and persecutors of religion.[44] This clash coincided with
early rumblings of the impending storm between Izetbegović and
Bosnian Prime Minister Haris Silajdžić, at the 6th session of the
General Council of the SDA on 18–19 January. To Silajdžić's
increasing restlessness in the face of the government's
marginalisation in affairs concerning the Army, Izetbegović would
respond by insisting that full authority over the latter be vested in
him as President of the Presidency.[45]

The Bosnian Military Revival

By mid-1994 a certain military equilibrium had been reached in the
Bosnian war. Serb forces held approximately 70% of the country;
Bosnian forces 20% and Croatian forces 10%. However, the
Bosnian Republic held the country's economic and demographic
heartland, with a population of about two million, as against 600,000

for the 'Serb Republic' and 200,000 for the HR H-B. The ARBiH possessed 110,000 troops organised in six corps with 100,000 reserves, as against 80,000 for the VRS and 50,000 for the HVO.[46] Between 1 March and 30 July the ARBiH succeeded in building a tunnel linking Sarajevo to the free territory outside the Serb encirclement, through which military units would immediately begin passing.[47] The ARBiH also underwent a significant reorganisation. The 6th (Konjic) Corps of the ARBiH was disbanded on 27 February 1994 and its units incorporated in the 4th (Mostar) Corps. The 7th (Travnik) Corps was established in April 1994 from units previously included in the 3rd (Zenica) Corps. Operational groups were formed from among the ARBiH's units at the start of 1994, as well as mobile battalions within the brigades. In the spring of 1995 the operational groups would be disbanded and mobile brigades and divisions formed.[48] However, the ARBiH remained seriously handicapped by its lack of heavy weapons: it possessed about 40 tanks and 30 APCs, as against 330 and 400 respectively for the VRS.[49] General Jovan Divjak, Deputy Commander of the ARBiH, stated in February 1995 that of over 200,000 Bosnian soldiers only 50,000 were armed; indeed 'not one of our units is fully armed because of the arms embargo.'[50]

The VRS's soldiers, however, suffered from very low morale, poor discipline and high rates of desertion, even among officers, and were incapable of defending their overextended front lines.[51] The VRS had been handicapped since the start of the war by a difference of military doctrine among its leaders: between a 'Partisan' line, as represented by Ratko Mladić and the General Staff, which favoured organisation on the basis of a unified command under professional officers, and a 'Chetnik' line, as represented by Karadžić and the SDS leaders, which favoured the autonomy of local 'Vojvodas' or warlords, based on their local political standing.[52] This division, which reflected similar divisions in the ARBiH, resulted in two parallel systems of military command in the VRS, which tied in with a growing power-struggle between Mladić and Karadžić. Offensive operations by the VRS required reinforcements from Serbia: the redeployment of forces for a counter-offensive against the 5th Corps at Bihać in the autumn of 1994 necessitated the mobilisation of 7,000 troops from Užice and Montenegro and their transferral to

East Bosnia;[53] and even the conquest of the isolated East Bosnian enclave of Srebrenica in July 1995 required the assistance of the Yugoslav Army.[54]

The ARBiH, which had at birth been essentially self-financed on the part of individual soldiers and therefore under-financed, now had a steady income for military expenditure: from April 1992 until June 1993, approximately three million Deutschmarks were expended on the ARBiH; from June until December 1993, over thirty-five million.[55] The ARBiH still suffered from serious incompetence at the highest levels, perhaps exacerbated by politicisation of the officer corps. In June 1994, in an operation reminiscent of Soviet tactics in the Russo-Finnish war of 1939–40, the Bosnians suffered at least two thousand casualties in an unsuccessful frontal offensive in the Ozren region in north-central Bosnia.[56] The HVO had ceased to fight the ARBiH, but had yet to deploy itself against the VRS; the turn of fortunes in the war would depend upon Croatian policy, itself dependent on the policy of the Great Powers. Although unwilling to break the arms embargo itself, the USA following the Washington Agreement had given the green light for an unlikely ally – Iran – to provide weapons to the ARBiH via Croatia.[57] Without the lifting of the arms embargo, however, the ARBiH would be unable to achieve a military victory without massive Croatian assistance. In the absence of the latter, it was condemned to fight a grinding war of attrition focussed on the struggle for control of roads, mountains and radar stations.[58] In 1941–45 the Partisans' political appeals to their enemies' soldiers on the basis of a multi-national Bosnia-Herzegovina had enabled them to capture even large towns in all parts of the country despite their poor armaments; the SDA regime's purely military strategy and inability to appeal to the Serb and Croat populations condemned it to military stalemate.

The military and diplomatic impasse was to be broken by the ARBiH's 5th Corps which, based in the Cazinska Krajina in the extreme north-west of Bosnia and wholly surrounded by Serb-occupied territory, had existed as a virtually autonomous army since the start of the war. The first units for resistance were established in the Cazinska Krajina, the most solidly Muslim area of Bosnia-Herzegovina, under the aegis of the PL and local SDA politicians in

September 1991. Serbian aggression against the region began on 21 April 1992 with an assault on Bosanska Krupa. By the end of August there existed a total of seven brigades in the Cazinska Krajina, united in the 'Una-Sana Operational Group' under the command of Ramiz Dreković, a PL member and former officer of the JNA. The Una-Sana Operational Group was transformed into the 5th Corps between 10 and 21 October 1992 following the September decision of the Bosnian Presidency on the formation of corps.[59] Its chief logistical support, however, would come from Croatia rather than from the Bosnian Army; a throwback to World War II, when the Partisans' 'Una Operational Group' in the Cazinska Krajina fought as part of the 'People's Liberation Army of Croatia'. Thus at the beginning of May 1992 the first flight took place of what would be termed the Zagreb-to-Bihać 'air bridge', carrying supplies from the Croatian capital to the besieged enclave (though Salko Begić, who organised the 'air bridge', states that while certain Croatian officers gave him invaluable support, Zagreb nevertheless insisted that the Bosnian state pay for all supplies provided).[60]

In September 1993 the northern part of the Cazinska Krajina centred on the town of Velika Kladuša became the scene of the most serious Muslim rebellion against the Bosnian government, led by Presidency member and Serb agent Fikret Abdić. Parts of two of the 5th Corps brigades mutinied and put themselves under Abdić's rebel command. On 21 October Boban, as 'President' of the HR H-B, signed an alliance with Abdić's 'Autonomous Province of West Bosnia' and attempted to place Bihać's small HVO unit under the command of Abdić's forces.[61] The Bihać Command of the HVO, however, refused to end cooperation with the 5th Corps, on the grounds that the Croats and Muslims of the area had no history of enmity and that the Croats wished to continue the struggle against the Serbo-Montenegrin aggressor.[62] Abdić's xenophobic media denounced Dreković as a native of the Sanjak region in Serbia, with no links to the Krajina; he was consequently replaced in November 1993 by Atif Dudaković as 5th Corps commander.[63]

Dudaković was to turn the 5th Corps into the spearhead of the ARBiH's military resurgence. On 7–9 July 1994, in a spectacular military ruse known as 'Operation Tiger', Dudaković staged a phoney rebellion among units of the 5th Corps, with the 502nd

Chivalrous Brigade faking a military attack on the 5th Corps HQ at Bihać.[64] Abdić's attempt to intervene on the side of the 'rebels' led to over-extension of his forces and their military collapse; his stronghold of Velika Kladuša fell to the 5th Corps on 21 August 1994. In September 1994 concerted attacks on the 5th Corps by Serb forces based in occupied Croatia and Bosanska Krajina were defeated. In the second of these, the VRS's Commander-in-Chief Ratko Mladić narrowly escaped capture, with the 5th Corps penetrating into occupied Croatia.[65] On 25–26 October the 5th Corps launched 'Grmeč '94', an offensive eastwards in the face of which local VRS forces crumbled. The stronghold of Grabež was captured along with large quantities of military equipment and, as Dudaković said at the time, 'Many Chetniks have left their bones forever in our forests.'[66]

The Serb front lines collapsed and the following days saw further capture of territory, villages and equipment, with reports that 'many of the aggressor's soldiers who will never again dream of Great Serbia were left on the battlefield.'[67] Grabež would remain in the hands of the 5th Corps throughout the war. Throughout these operations the Bihać HVO loyally defended the 5th Corps's rear from the forces of the RSK.[68] The 5th Corps surrounded the VRS-held town of Bosanska Krupa and pushed south to the town of Kulen Vakuf.

These successes of the 5th Corps, although transitory, alerted public opinion in Bosnia-Herzegovina and Croatia to the sorry state of the Serb armed forces. On 3 November, in the first successful joint operation between the HVO and the ARBiH since the Washington Agreement of March, Serb forces were driven out of Kupres. The autumn of 1994 would see the ARBiH recapture much of the territory around Sarajevo it had lost to the VRS the previous summer: Igman, Bjelašnica, Treskavica and territory around Trnovo. The capture in September of Igman, a supposedly 'demilitarised zone', prompted UN commander Michael Rose to threaten air-strikes against the ARBiH. At the end of November the Croatian Army began a major offensive in the Livno valley region of south-west Bosnia, aimed at outflanking rebel-Serb forces in occupied Croatia. Nevertheless, the VRS responded to the 5th Corps successes with a counter-offensive involving an attack on the rear of the Bihać pocket by RSK forces from occupied Croatia, that succeeded in recapturing most of the lost territory, reinstalled Fikret Abdić in his Velika Kladuša stronghold and threatened to take Bihać. Although successful in the short term, this Serb effort proved to be the equivalent of the German U-boat offensive in World War I: a military gamble that provoked the formation of an invincible opposing coalition in response, in this case between Croatia and Bosnia-Herzegovina with the blessing of the USA.[69] The Serb counter-offensive furthermore failed to regain the military initiative for the floundering VRS. In March 1995 the ARBiH went on the offensive again, breaking a UN ceasefire to capture the strategically crucial Mt Vlašić in Central Bosnia with its key relay station and attacking unsuccessfully another key Serb relay station at Stolice in north-east Bosnia.

Izetbegović vs Silajdžić

Whereas the Army had by 1994–95 long since ceased to play any political as opposed to military role in the struggle for a unified Bosnia-Herzegovina, its political role in the maintenance of the SDA regime was increasingly important at the expense of its military performance. On 15 April 1994, at the height of the battle for Goražde, Commander Delić spent the entire day holding conferences in celebration of the second anniversary of the ARBiH's birth, and spent the evening with his top commanders at the theatre in Sarajevo.[70] Major military operations would be undertaken less for strategic reasons than for the sake of the regime's political ambitions or to improve its political standing. 7th Corps commander General Mehmed Alagić, himself an SDA supporter, recalls Izetbegović demanding he break the siege of Maglaj, even though this was not militarily feasible.[71] Alagić subsequently resisted Izetbegović's surrender of strategically key territory around Kupres to the HVO, as part of an agreement on 'borders' with Croatian President Tuđman.[72] Far more costly would be the ARBiH's attempt to break the siege of Sarajevo in June and July 1995, undertaken without the requisite military conditions, which may have cost the lives of over four hundred Bosnian soldiers. In the face of the exhaustion of Sarajevo's population and the unwillingness of the Western alliance to confront Serbia, Izetbegović had spoken openly, on repeated occasions beginning in April 1995, of attempting to break the siege militarily. The offensive was undertaken for political reasons: to stabilise the regime and reassert its credibility.[73] According to Alagić, 'The President felt perpetually afraid because the tunnel was the only way out of Sarajevo, and urged us to hurry with breaking the siege'; so prior to the offensive Izetbegović announced he would not leave the capital until the siege had been lifted.[74] At the same time Commander Delić would in early July call for 'common and coordinated activity' of the Party and Army to ensure favourable conditions on the home front during the offensive.[75] This military operation was notable also for the role played by the Kiseljak HVO, which was due to participate in the offensive but arranged with Serb forces to stage a phoney Croat military victory that would be filmed as proof of the HVO's adherence to the alliance with the ARBiH.[76]

The counterpart to the Sarajevo offensive was the abandonment of the besieged enclaves of Srebrenica and Žepa in East Bosnia to Serb forces in July. Izetbegović, Ganić and other SDA leaders had discussed handing over Srebrenica and Žepa to the VRS on several occasions, in exchange for Serb abandonment of the occupied Sarajevo suburbs of Vogošća and Ilijaš that separated the capital from the rest of government-held territory.[77] In March 1995 Naser Orić, commander of the 28th Division in Srebrenica, and fifteen of his officers were withdrawn from the enclave for 'retraining' and never returned; yet in June the defenders of Srebrenica were required to launch diversionary attacks on the VRS in support of the offensive around Sarajevo, a tactic General Divjak condemned as 'insane' since it provided justification for the Serb counter-offensive and occupation of the 'safe area'.[78] The order to launch diversionary attacks was for this reason resisted by the commander of the ARBiH's 28th Division in the enclave. While insisting on diversionary attacks from Srebrenica, the Staff of the 2nd Corps moved its elite units *away* from Srebrenica and towards Sarajevo, a mere four days before the enclave fell. 2nd Corps commander Sead

Delić resisted all calls from his officers for a military push to link up with soldiers and civilians fleeing from Srebrenica.[79] On 11 July, the day the VRS occupied the town, Rasim Delić devoted only five minutes of his twenty-five minute military report to this imminent military catastrophe. The SDA leadership also ignored the latter, preoccupied as it was with finding a replacement for 'Vice-President' Ganić who had been injured in a road accident.[80] This was despite the fact that the VRS's conquest of Srebrenica was followed by the cold-blooded massacre of at least 7,000 Muslim men and boys. The ARBiH General Staff made no military effort whatsoever to assist Srebrenica, for whose survival the regime chose to rely solely on the international community. Delić subsequently blamed Srebrenica's fall on the incompetence of its defenders. Izetbegović admitted that the town could have held out for a further month had it received the support of the Army.[81] Naser Orić accuses the Bosnian regime of having deliberately sacrificed the enclave; his own prior power struggle with the SDA for control of the town may help to explain the failure of coordination between him and the commanders of the General Staff and the 2nd Corps.[82] The fall of Srebrenica was followed by the VRS's conquest of Žepa on 25 July, an event that received even less attention from the Bosnian leadership and from the Western powers.

The failed Sarajevo offensive and the fall of Srebrenica provided the occasion for a showdown between Izetbegović and Silajdžić, who resigned as Prime Minister on 3 August. The latter, whose Muslim-national orientation was scarcely less pronounced than that of the President, had nevertheless opposed the public announcement of the start of the Sarajevo offensive and was aggrieved that major military operations of this kind were undertaken without his consultation.[83] He had favoured reduction of the 210,000–strong conscript army by at least 50,000 and its transformation into a professional force; this may have conflicted with the hardline-SDA vision of the Army as an incubator of national and religious consciousness among the Muslim 'nation in arms'.[84] In the view of General Sakib Mahmuljin, commander of the 3rd Corps, in November 1995:

We are still not a professional army. We are a people's army. To be precise, we are a nation in uniform. It is not, surely, a sin to engage in politics in uniform while we wage resistance against our biological and political disappearance. Mr Ganić has said that he joined the Party of Democratic Action in the belief that through it he could do most to help his nation. I am of the same opinion.[85]

Silajdžić's other demands also concerned the Army: dissolution of military in favour of civilian administration in parts of the country, and revitalisation of the Military Council of the Republic. Upon resigning, he denounced the Sarajevo offensive for preparing the ground for the Serb conquest of Srebrenica and Žepa.[86] At the SDA General Council meeting of 5 August in Zenica, which censured Silajdžić following his resignation, Čengić hit back at him by denouncing the entire role of the government in Bosnia-Herzegovina's defences:

The attitude of the Government points to the creation of a pacifist atmosphere in a situation in which we are constantly exposed to aggression. The Ministry of Defence, with the premier's support, these days attempts to break the unity of the functioning of the defence system and commands the defence from the Ministry of Defence of Croatia, at a time when we have our own line of supply and when from that line of supply we give a significant percentage every time to the Ministry of Defence of Croatia.[87]

If Čengić's concerns were sincere, it would appear that far from reintegrating the Bosnian state the Washington Agreement had accelerated its partition and the transformation of the ARBiH into a Party army. The integration of the Ministry of Defence into a joint Croatian-Bosnian defensive system led Izetbegović and the SDA leadership to sideline their own government so as to protect the Army from Croatian influence. When Prime Minister Silajdžić reacted by resigning, the very Bosnian government itself would come under fire as an enemy of a state that was increasingly identified solely with the President, Party and Army. At the SDA General Council meeting of 5 August Izetbegović received messages of 'unreserved support' from many ARBiH units, including the 7th Muslim Brigade and the Black Swans.[88] The secretary of the SDA's Srebrenica organisation, however, subsequently accused his President and party leader of deliberate betrayal of the enclave and defected to Silajdžić's new party in protest.[89]

Following the Council's censure of the premier, a directive was sent to all members of the ARBiH instructing them on the appropriate reaction to the crisis. Carrying Rasim Delić's signature, it was in fact written by Muslimović as Chief of the Department for Morale of the General Staff. The directive claimed:

> *Silajdžić's conduct does great damage and incites enemy propaganda against our liberation struggle. Silajdžić's conduct wholly conforms to the consistent, well-known efforts of our enemies to sow dissension and conflict among the highest political and state leaders of our country. It is precisely this that gives Silajdžić's conduct its thoughtless, deceitful and irresponsible character.*

In this way Muslimović demonised the Bosnian Prime Minister among his own troops by equating him with 'our enemies'. Furthermore:

> *To understand fully the causes of Silajdžić's resignation it must be borne in mind that he had ambitions to take over functions that are not within the jurisdiction of the Premier, particularly as concerns the organisation of our defence and the command of the Army of the RBiH. He frequently requested the radical reduction of the size of the Army of the RBiH, which would threaten our defences and our liberation struggle. In addition to this, Silajdžić failed to carry out the duties of the Government in the field of material supplies for members of the Army of RBiH. He did not show concern in the field of resolving important questions and problems related to invalids and the wounded. He delayed the passing of a law concerning the pay of members of the RBiH.*

Muslimović thus sought to present Silajdžić's proposals for military reform in treasonous terms, and accused him at the same time of threatening the soldiers' and veterans' livelihoods. The clinching argument was that 'Silajdžić's conduct was unanimously condemned at the extended session of the General Council of the SDA ...' The directive ended with a reminder that 'the basis of orientation' for members of the ARBiH should be 'the demands of our Supreme Commander President of the Presidency Mr Alija Izetbegović.'[90] Muslimović subsequently described Silajdžić publicly as 'the greatest enemy of the Bosniaks'.[91] For this former military intelligence officer of a Communist regime, the Army had to be immunised against the influence of a high-ranking official who had violated the discipline of the Party.

The Final Offensives

The remaining four months of the war, in which the VRS was brought to the verge of complete collapse and the ARBiH liberated a large part of the country, ironically saw Bosnia-Herzegovina's fate decided more than ever by foreign powers, especially the USA and Croatia. The Serb conquest of Srebrenica was followed by Milošević's last gamble on a military victory, through the destruction of the 5th Corps and the conquest of Bihać and the Cazinska Krajina, which would be attempted by General Mile Mrkšić, newly appointed by Belgrade for the purpose and operating from Serb-occupied Croatia. In response, Izetbegović and Tuđman signed an agreement on 22 July at Split for military cooperation, according to which, on the grounds of the 'ineffectiveness of the international community', it was stated that the 'Republic and Federation of Bosnia-Herzegovina called upon the Republic of Croatia to extend military and other assistance to their defence against aggression, especially in the Bihać area, which the Republic of Croatia has accepted.'[92] Consequently on 28–29 July the Croatian Army captured the towns of Bosansko Grahovo and Glamoč from the VRS, cutting communications between Knin and Banja Luka. On 4–7 August the Croatian Army – with 5th Corps assistance – destroyed the RSK and liberated all territory held by Serb forces in central Croatia. The armaments captured by the 5th Corps in the process would bestow upon it an offensive capability that the rest of the ARBiH would not possess during the remainder of the war. A tactical bonus was handed to the allies when NATO belatedly launched its first serious air-strikes of the war, beginning on 30 August, which knocked out the VRS's communications system and left it 'deaf and blind' – though the NATO action did not target the area of Bosanska Krajina where the offensive was taking place.[93] The military significance of these strikes has often been exaggerated by Western commentators: as US Air Force Chief of Staff General Ronald Fogleman stated at the time, the purpose of the strikes was to 'have reduced the overall Serb ability to conduct further offensive operations, while leaving enough supplies for front-line troops to defend themselves against opportunistic aggression [by the Croatians and Bosnians].'[94]

A full scale offensive by the Croatian Army and the ARBiH in Bosanska Krajina in September destroyed the VRS's 2nd Krajina Corps and liberated seven towns. The Croatian Army in 'Operation Maestral' took Drvar, Šipovo and Jajce; the 5th Corps in 'Operation Sana' took Bosanski Petrovac, Ključ and Bosanska Krupa and the 7th Corps took Donji Vakuf. The allies threatened to capture Banja Luka and put an end to the Serb Republic's existence west of the Brčko corridor. To the east, the 2nd and 3rd Corps advanced in Ozren, liberating Vozuća and threatening Doboj. These operations made a 'reality on the ground' of the distribution of territory between the combatants favoured by the Great Powers, according to which 51% of Bosnia-Herzegovina was to go to the Federation and 49% to the 'Serb Republic'. Nevertheless, the US did not wish the allies actually to defeat the 'Serb Republic', merely to cut it down to size. All manner of diplomatic and military means were brought to bear by the West on the Croatians and Bosnians to halt their offensive. Allied military operations were also hampered by the continuing hostility of the Tuđman regime to its nominal Bosnian allies.[95] Accordingly, on 19 September the offensive was halted under intense Western and particularly US pressure. The respite allowed the VRS to stabilise its lines and to launch a counter-offensive in early October, threatening the newly liberated towns of Ključ and Bosanska Krupa; but the attack was defeated with the assistance of 7th Corps troops transferred into Bosanska Krajina across Croatian-held territory. Izetbegović signed a conditional cease-fire on 5 October, but the Bosnian forces nevertheless resumed their offensive in Western Bosnia, leading on 10 October to the capture of Mrkonjić Grad by the Croatian Army and Sanski Most by the 5th Corps. The notorious so-called 'Tigers' paramilitary force of Željko Raznatović-Arkan – which had been sent from Serbia to stiffen Bosnian Serb morale but had been caught up in Karadžić's feud with Mladić, producing havoc among the Serb forces – was routed at Sanski Most.[96] Following these final Bosnian victories, a lasting cease-fire was signed on the 12th. In total two-sevenths of occupied Bosnia-Herzegovina had been liberated; the liberation of Vozuća territorially linked the 2nd and 3rd Corps and the industrial centres of Tuzla and Zenica; the liberation of Donji Vakuf reopened the main highway between Zenica and the Croatian coast; and the allies had come within 20km of Banja Luka.

These operations may have witnessed a difference in policy between the ambitious commanders of the 5th and 7th Corps, Generals Dudaković and Alagić, on the one hand and Izetbegović on the other. In the weeks before the cease-fire the generals had planned to take the VRS-held towns of Prijedor and Bosanski Novi and to win the war by capturing Banja Luka, the largest Serb-held city in Bosnia-Herzegovina, an intention that Dudaković had publicly announced.[97] Dudaković and Alagić stated further that 'Our goal remains the River Drina', i.e. the internationally recognised border between Bosnia-Herzegovina and Serbia.[98] They were therefore reluctant to cease fighting. The ARBiH resumed offensive actions on 12–13 October aimed at capturing the symbolically important town of Prijedor, scene of some of the worst Serb atrocities against Muslims in 1992, as well as Omarska, site of the most infamous Serb concentration camp. This raised accusations of 'disobedient generals' defying their president's order for a cease-fire. Muhamed Borogovac has suggested that Izetbegović and Delić were forced to 'discipline' the West Bosnian generals. General Vahid Karavelić, the overall Bosnian commander during the autumn operations in West Bosnia and an Izetbegović loyalist, was used by Izetbegović, Borogovac suggests, to reign in the West Bosnian generals.[99] Dudaković subsequently stated: 'If there had been more time and units, we should certainly have liberated more territory. However, following the signing of the Agreement, we received the order 'STOP, military operations are halted'.[100] According to the journalist Šefko Hodžić, who was present at Dudaković's and Alagić's staff when Karavelić arrived with the order for the final cession of operations, the West Bosnian generals were 'frankly furious at having to halt their military operations'.[101] Izetbegović recalls that 'the soldiers, particularly natives of Krajina [West Bosnia] Dudaković and Alagić, were not overjoyed at the reaching of a cease-fire.'[102] Nevertheless, it appears that the alleged clash between Izetbegović on the one hand and Dudaković and Alagić on the other may have been staged to enable the capture of Prijedor, Omarska and Bosanski Novi without the Bosnian leadership appearing to violate the cease-fire. This was itself a product of the ambiguous US position on the war. For while the sympathies of the US administration were with the Bosnian side, nevertheless US policy was to stop the war on the basis of the 'Contact Group Plan' awarding 49% of Bosnian territory to the Serb side, this being a product of British and French diplomacy that had favoured the Serb side since the start of the war. Clinton wished to halt the war, not help the Bosnians to win it; he ultimately challenged the Anglo-French means of bringing this about – through appeasing the Serbs – but never the Anglo-French model for a peace settlement. US envoy Richard Holbrooke was therefore ready, as a goodwill gesture toward the Bosnians, to give them a couple of days grace to take Prijedor, Bosanski Novi and Omarska, but not to permit them to endanger the cease-fire or to threaten Banja Luka. Nevertheless, the Bosnian troops were too exhausted to take the territories permitted to them in so short an interval.[103]

The question remains as to why Izetbegović should have agreed to a cease-fire precisely when the ARBiH was on the verge of a spectacular victory. Izetbegović was undoubtedly under heavy pressure to desist from the Americans, whom he claims went so far as to threaten the ARBiH with air-strikes in the event that they marched on Banja Luka:

We could have achieved a military victory against the Chetniks in October 1995. We were stopped. We could have taken Prijedor. Most probably we could have driven them out of Banja Luka if we had continued the offensive, because they were in complete disarray. However, in practical terms the USA stopped this war … we were virtually given an ultimatum to stop, and they said they would begin to carry out strikes on us if we continued the offensive …[104]

It did not occur to Izetbegović to call the Americans' bluff and attack Banja Luka regardless. Izetbegović's calculations were undoubtedly affected by a diminution of military support from the Croatian Army, Tuđman having no desire to see Serbia defeated or the Bosnian state rejuvenated. As Izetbegović recalls, 'Tuđman threatened openly that not a single bullet for Bosnia would any longer be permitted to cross his territory.'[105] Waging war with an ally as treacherous as Tuđman was inherently problematic. The Split Agreement of 22 July had entrusted the administration of liberated territory to whichever army captured it, leading to inevitable rivalry and lapses in cooperation between the Bosnian and Croatian forces.[106] The priority given by Izetbegović to the diplomatic front thus left the progress of the ARBiH's offensive at the mercy of Bosnian relations with Croatia and the USA. A few more days of resistance to the Western powers' *diktat* could nevertheless have enabled the ARBiH to take Bosanski Novi, Prijedor and Omarska, as well as the strategically crucial town of Doboj in north-central Bosnia. Izetbegović's disregard of the situation on the battlefield is illustrated by the fact that it was only after the cease-fire that he, by his own account, asked Dudaković to 'Tell me, please, whether you were able to enter Banja Luka?', to which Dudaković allegedly replied 'I was not!', whereupon Izetbegović responded 'Ah, now I feel better about it!'.[107] Nevertheless, Izetbegović's acceptance of a cease-fire on the eve of victory may have been motivated as much by internal as external causes. The most important factor in his decision may have been that he had long since abandoned any hope in a military victory and reconciled himself to some degree of partition. The cease-fire, leaving half of Bosnia-Herzegovina in Serb hands, was therefore in his eyes a success rather than a failure.

The military operations of September and October 1995 represent a judgement on the military and political project of the Izetbegović regime: despite the ARBiH's valiant effort across three and a half years of war, in the final victorious offensive the 1st, 2nd, 3rd and 4th Corps captured no towns of any size while the 7th Corps captured the single town of Donji Vakuf, and that only when the VRS was anyway withdrawing to avoid being outflanked by the Croatian Army advancing through Jajce. The 5th Corps, territorially separated from the Bosnian government's heartland and thus a virtually distinct army, captured four towns in 'Operation Sana', of which Sanski Most was liberated with assistance from other corps. When the Croatian effort lagged during the second half of September, even these gains were threatened. Furthermore, the 5th Corps's effort to liberate the town of Bosanski Novi was unsuccessful, in part due to the lawless nature of the Bosnian rear, with soldiers deserting the front lines to participate in the plunder and appropriation of real estate in liberated Bosanska Krupa.[108] On the other hand, the VRS was in a state of collapse. Recruited on the basis of a 'people in arms', its ideology was that of loyalty to Belgrade and Serbia rather than defence of any given portion of Bosnian territory. Unlike the Croatian Army in Vukovar or the ARBiH in Bihać, Goražde and elsewhere, the VRS in 1995 made no attempt to engage in street fighting in defence of towns surrounded by the advancing enemy forces. Once the enemy captured the strategic points surrounding a town, the VRS would withdraw to avoid encirclement.[109] Its officers were fighting not for their homes but for the dream of a Great Serbia, for which they would not fight to the death. At the same time the VRS did not possess the cohesiveness of a regular army: if a Serb village came under artillery attack, Serb soldiers from the village would desert the VRS to return home to protect their families.[110] The 2nd Krajina Corps collapsed in part due to demoralising rumours among its troops that the southern part of Bosanska Krajina was being abandoned to the Muslims and Croats by Serb politicians as part of a peace agreement. The 'Serb Republic's' leaders were placing their hopes of survival in the international community.[111]

Even without Croatian support, the ARBiH's military position at the end of 1995 was far better than it had been in August-September 1993, when the Izetbegovic regime had rejected the 'Owen-Stoltenberg Peace Plan' to continue its offensive against the HR H-B. Yet the territory left to the Izetbegović regime by Dayton was approximately equal in extent to that offered by Owen-Stoltenberg, or approximately 30% of the territory of Bosnia-Herzegovina. Owen-Stoltenberg had awarded Doboj, Srebrenica, Žepa, Stolac and the Croat-held enclaves in Central Bosnia to the projected Muslim entity, all of which would under Dayton go to the Serb Republic or the HVO. By contrast, Dayton left to the ARBiH the territory liberated by the 5th Corps in 'Operation Sana', centred on the towns of Bosanski Petrovac, Ključ and Sanski Most. In other words, the Izetbegović regime had rejected a territorial settlement in September 1993 in order to fight another two years for one that was, outside of 5th Corps territory, *less* favourable to it. But Owen-Stoltenberg had threatened to place Sarajevo under UN administration and grant the Serb and Croat entities the eventual right to secede; the Izetbegović regime's political gains in the two years following its rejection of Owen-Stoltenberg were unimpeded control of the capital and the *de jure* preservation of a Bosnia-Herzegovina partitioned *de facto*.

Conclusion

The Dayton Accord of November 1995 was signed by Izetbegović and Silajdžić only under intense US pressure, but should nevertheless be taken as the logical culmination of the policy of the SDA regime. The 'Serb Republic' was recognised as a virtually independent entity and the VRS left as a separate army in control of 49% of Bosnia-Herzegovina. The ARBiH and the HVO were to be united in a Federation Army from corps level upwards to the Joint Command, leaving the lower units wholly separate. The HVO consequently remained in control of approximately 20% of Bosnian territory. The Western Alliance was to 'arm and train' the Bosnian Army, but the latter's forces were to be greatly reduced and set at a level inferior to that of its opponents. Annex 1B of the Dayton Agreement set the ratio of armaments between Bosnia-Herzegovina, Croatia and Serbia at 2:2:5. One-third of Bosnian armaments was allocated to the VRS and two-thirds to the Federation Army, giving Serb forces a superiority of 17:10 over Bosnian and Croatian forces combined. The Federation Army's armaments were to be divided between the ARBiH and HVO according to subsequent negotiations, meaning that a significant portion of the 'Bosnian' armed forces would be under the influence of Zagreb rather than Sarajevo. Furthermore, Dayton left territory under ARBiH control that in many places was not strategically viable. Sarajevo was to be reunited and given a solid territorial link to the rest of ARBiH territory, through Serb surrender of the suburbs of Vogošća, Ilijaš and Ilidža. Sarajevo would remain a frontline city, however, with Serb forces immediately to the east and south, and in possession of the peak of Mt Trebević from which they would be able to shell the capital in the event of a renewed conflict. The last eastern enclave of Goražde was to be given a tenuous territorial link to the rest of ARBiH-controlled territory, but remained strategically unviable. The Cazinska Krajina was once again to be cut off from Central Bosnia, by Croatian surrender to the Serb Republic of the so-called 'anvil' of territory around Šipovo and Mrkonjić-Grad. The strategically crucial town of Doboj was to remain in the Serb Republic, despite having been promised to the Federation under the Contact Group Peace Plan of July 1994. The fate of Brčko, the most strategically important town of all, was to be decided by international arbitration and would remain in the meantime under Serb control.[1] The 'Serb Republic' was recognised by the Izetbegović regime in November 1995, when the latter was on the verge of military victory, rather than in September 1993 when it had been on the verge of defeat; the Izetbegović regime accelerated the partition of Bosnia-Herzegovina politically and ethnically even as the ARBiH struggled to reverse the partition militarily and territorially. But while Dayton represented the sacrifice of Bosnia-Herzegovina's military interests to the political interests of the regime, it nevertheless guaranteed perpetual Muslim domination of the Bosnian heartland, including three and a half of the country's five largest cities. The Muslim population of Bosnia-Herzegovina had been protected from genocide and won a genuine degree of security under international protection, and refugees from East Bosnia would find new homes in the Sarajevo suburbs newly emptied of their Serb population. The campaign waged by the ARBiH was unsuccessful as a Bosnian-Herzegovinian liberation struggle, except insofar as Bosnia-Herzegovina's independence was formally recognised by Serbia, Croatia and the international community; it was successful, however, as a Muslim-Bosniak national-liberation struggle.

In 1989 Bosnia-Herzegovina had been garrisoned by a decentralised multi-national Territorial Defence, under the leadership of the League of Communists of Bosnia-Herzegovina. In

1995 largely the same officers and soldiers continued to garrison the country, but the latter's military forces had been violently reordered as three centralised, ethnically pure armies, each in control of an ethnically homogenous territory. Each of the three armies has remained politically loyal to a single nationalist party, made up in large part of former Communists. The decentralisation of the Bosnian armed forces had been solved by the Izetbegović regime through their transformation into a Party army subject to a small number of top leaders, most notably Hasan Čengić and Izetbegović himself. This had involved a series of political or military conflicts with local political rivals: the HVO and the HDZ in Croat-inhabited areas; the criminal forces of Prazina, Topalović and Delalić in Sarajevo; the Social Democratic authorities in Tuzla; Fikret Abdić in the Cazinska Krajina and Naser Orić in Srebrenica. The SDA's political project left it as the undisputed master in ARBiH territory at the war's end. The establishment of what was effectively a Muslim parastate disguised by the figleaf of the Federation was a defensive measure in the face of Great Serbian and Great Croatian aggression and genocide against Bosnia-Herzegovina and the Muslims. It also, however, made the SDA an accomplice of the project to partition Bosnia-Herzegovina along ethnic lines.

Bin Laden in the Balkans? The Bosnian Army and the *Mujahedin*

The terrorist attack against New York and Washington on 11 September 2001 has inevitably focussed interest retrospectively on the role of foreign *mujahedin* in the war in Bosnia-Herzegovina and the alleged involvement of Osama bin Laden himself. During the war a trickle of right-wing extremists, mercenaries and adventurers joined the struggle on opposing sides, with Russians, Greeks, French, Belgians and other Europeans fighting on the Serbian and Croatian sides and volunteers from the Islamic world – and even a few principled idealists from Christian Europe and elsewhere – joining the Bosnians. Informed estimates of the numbers of *mujahedin* who fought on the side of the ARBiH range from a few hundreds to up to three thousand; wild Serbian and Croatian claims of tens of thousands of fanatical bearded Arabs flooding into Bosnia-Herzegovina were a product of the propaganda war of the time rather than a reflection of reality. Izetbegović said of the *mujahedin*, following the 11 September atrocities: 'We never invited them. We didn't, in fact, need them. We had 200,000 people ready to fight. What we needed was arms. And we specifically didn't need people whose origins we didn't know.'[1] Given the partial collapse of the Bosnian state and the ad hoc character of Bosnian armed forces in many areas, however, many *mujahedin* were able to arrive on the front lines and participate in the fighting on a basis that was autonomous from the official ARBiH command structure.

The difficulty in reaching many areas of Bosnia-Herzegovina led to a concentration of the *mujahedin* in Central Bosnia, where the HVO bore the brunt of their activities during 1993. The *mujahedin* fell under the formal jurisdiction of the 7th Muslim Brigade of the 3rd Corps, alongside which they fought. The ARBiH Supreme Command Staff eventually moved to incorporate the *mujahedin* formally into its command structure and on 13 August 1993 ordered the establishment of the El Mujahed Detachment, into which all foreign fighters were supposed to be organised. This unit was initially placed under the direct command of the Staff of the 3rd Corps and on 6 September under the Operational Group for Bosanska Krajina. During 1993 *muhahedin* were allegedly involved in the killing and torture of Croat and Serb civilians and prisoners of war within the framework of ARBiH operations. On 5 July 2001 the ICTY indicted former commander of the 3rd Corps Major-General Enver Hadžihasanović, former commander of the Bosanska Krajina Operational Group Brigadier-General Mehmed Alagić and former commander of the 7th Muslim Brigade Colonel Amir Kubura for war crimes related in part to the activities of the *mujahedin*.[2]

The foreign *mujahedin* were required to leave Bosnia-Herzegovina under the terms of the Dayton Accord. A total of about 70 foreign-born *mujahedin*, however, had received Bosnian citizenship during and after the war, some through marriage to Bosnian women, and a couple of hundred more may have remained illegally. Several of these were arrested as terrorist suspects in Bosnia-Herzegovina both before and after the 11 September attacks. Although the US and UK embassies in Sarajevo were briefly closed in October 2001 for fear of Islamist terrorist attacks, to date Western personnel or institutions have not been the objects of such attacks in Bosnia-Herzegovina, nor have any al-Qaʿida training camps been discovered there.[3] And while British, French and American citizens have joined al-Qaʿida or engaged in acts of Islamist terrorism internationally, not a single Bosnian Muslim is known to have done so. All this would be truly remarkable if 'an elaborate Islamic terror network' really had existed in Bosnia, as one Serb writer has claimed.[4] A number of *mujahedin* settled after the war in the Serb village of Bočinja Donja near Maglaj in Central Bosnia, which they captured from the VRS in

September 1995 and from which the Serb inhabitants fled or were expelled.[5] At Bočinja Donja former *mujahedin* on two occasions physically assaulted US soldiers of the Stabilisation Force (SFOR) attempting to repatriate Serb civilians to the village.[6] Physical violence of this kind, however, has been the response of members of all Bosnia-Herzegovina's ethnic groups to the attempted return of refugees and has no relation to Islamist terrorism. SFOR has since evicted most of the *mujahedin* from Bočinja Donja. Insofar as it cannot be excluded that al-Qa'ida ever had a presence in Bosnia-Herzegovina, this is hardly exceptional by European standards; as the international community's High Representative in Bosnia-Herzegovina Wolfgang Petritsch pointed out in November 2001, 'after all, the organisation had a base in Hamburg'.[7]

Of greater concern to Western intelligence than the alleged al-Qa'ida connections of the Bosnian Muslim political establishment has been the sale and distribution of Bosnian passports to foreign nationals, some of whom are suspected of having been al-Qa'ida activists who used them to travel in the context of their illegal activities.[8] The Sarajevo weekly *Dani* published an article on 24 September 1999 claiming that bin Laden himself was issued a Bosnian passport by the Bosnian Embassy in Vienna.[9] Yet there is no evidence that bin Laden ever visited Bosnia-Herzegovina or that he directed the activities of the *mujahedin* there, though it appears he may have visited Albania in 1994. The presence of the *mujahedin* in Bosnia-Herzegovina and their acquisition of Bosnian passports was a product of the collapse of the Bosnian state and the corruption of its institutions and officials, rather than of any alleged Islamist agenda on the part of the Izetbegović regime. Izetbegović for his part claims that he met with thousands of individuals from the Islamic world during the war in Bosnia-Herzegovina, and that he has no recollection of having met either bin Laden or his deputy Ayman al-Zawahiri; 'And if, by some chance, I have met them, then they could not have talked with me about terrorism.'[10] The Izetbegović regime did, however, enjoy close relations with the Islamic Republic of Iran, which helped arm the ARBiH during the war and which maintained an intelligence presence in Bosnia-Herzegovina following the signing of the Dayton Accord. In February 1996 the NATO-led

Implementation Force (IFOR) closed a training camp at Pogorelica near Fojnica at which Iranian intelligence officers had been engaged in training members of the Bosnian security services. IFOR arrested three Iranian intelligence officers and eight Bosnians in the process and seized stocks of arms. While NATO spoke of the Pogorelica camp as a 'terrorist training camp', the Bosnian Interior Ministry claimed it was an 'anti-terrorist centre' at which members of the Bosnian security services had received legitimate training for the purpose of arresting war criminals.[11] The planned activities of those trained at Pogorelica may have been directed against internal opponents of the Izetbegović regime.[12] There is no evidence, however, that they involved preparations for acts of terrorism against Western forces or institutions. The IFOR assault on the Pogorelica camp marked the definite end of the peculiar Iranian-US alliance of convenience over Bosnia-Herzegovina.

The 11 September attack inevitably provided a golden opportunity for enemies of Bosnia-Herzegovina, above all from the ranks of the Serb nationalists and right-wing and left-wing fundamentalists in the West, to equate the Izetbegović regime and the Bosnian Army with the fanatic Islamists of al-Qa'ida. This version of events upholds the popular stereotype of bin Laden as a master villain on the model of James Bond's arch-enemy Ernst Stavro Blofeld, at the head of an organisation similar to 'SPECTRE' with tentacles all over the world, one of which was allegedly linked to the Izetbegović regime, a second to the Kosovo Liberation Army and a third to the ethnic-Albanian National Liberation Army in Macedonia. Such a conflation of the moderate and radical sections of the Islamic world ultimately says more about the anti-Islamic prejudices of Western and other observers than it does about the Bosnian reality. Thus the Serbian state newspaper *Politika* claimed: 'After a secret agreement between Osama bin Laden and Alija Izetbegović, a Muslim state government took power in Sarajevo in 1994, four years before the Taliban came to power in Kabul, also with the help of the Saudi conspirator', ignoring the fact that under Izetbegović's alleged 'Muslim state government' the Bosnian state remained secular and women continued to participate in all walks of public life and to walk the Bosnian capital in miniskirts.[13]

A whole series of conspiracies have been alleged in relation to the former Yugoslavia: the 'German conspiracy' to engineer Croatia's secession from Yugoslavia; the 'Western media conspiracy' to 'demonise the Serbs' so as to justify Western military intervention; the 'US-NATO conspiracy' to 'fabricate' the Raçak massacre of Albanian civilians in Kosovo in January 1999, then to 'provoke' Serbia into rejecting the Rambouillet Accord the following month so as to justify the Kosovo War, with the ultimate motive of occupying Kosovo and building an oil pipeline through it; and so on. The 'Bosnia – bin Laden' conspiracy theory belongs to this category of the farcical. Indicative of the tendentious character of this conspiracy theory is the fact that one Western commentator for an 'anti-war' website, who wrote after 11 September of the 'extensive financial, ideological and military ties that linked Osama to the Bosnian government', was also claiming in the same period that the Israelis had foreknowledge of the attack on New York and Washington and laughed as the Twin Towers burned.[14] The reality was somewhat different: Islamists such as bin Laden were no more successful in conquering Bosnia-Herzegovina spiritually than was Milošević in conquering it through force of arms.

Notes

Introduction
1. This author fully respects the right of the Bosniak people to call themselves by whatever name they wish. However, since this historical account begins in the Communist era when the Bosniaks were still officially called Muslims, we have chosen for the sake of convenience to use the latter name throughout the text when referring to Bosnia-Herzegovina's largest constituent nation, except where the context requires otherwise.

Chapter 1
1. Archive of the Military-Historical Institute, Belgrade; NDH Collection, box 156, facsimile 6, document 38.
2. Attila Hoare, 'The People's Liberation Movement in Bosnia and Hercegovina, 1941–45: What Did It Mean to Fight for a Multi-National State?', *Nationalism and Ethnic Politics*, Vol. 2, No. 3, autumn 1996, pp. 418–423, 432–439 and *passim*.
3. James Gow, *Legitimacy and the Military: The Yugoslav Crisis*, 1992, pp. 43–45.
4. Milan Inđić, *Teritorijalna odbrana Socijalističke Republike Bosne i Hercegovine*, Republički stab Teritorijalna Odbrana Socijalistička Republika Bosna i Hercegovina, Sarajevo, 1989, pp. 30–41.
5. Ibid., pp. 54–55.
6. Ibid., pp. 81–82.
7. Ibid., pp. 146–7.
8. Hasim Efendić, *Ko je branio Bosnu*, OKO, Sarajevo, 1998, p. 214.
9. Branko Mamula, *Slučaj Jugoslaviija*, CID, Podgorica, 2000, p. 61.

10. Veljko Kadijević, *Moje viđenje raspada*, Politika, Belgrade, 1993, p. 77.
11. Ibid., p. 78.
12. Efendić, pp. 90–94.
13. Ibid., pp. 104–106.
14. Ibid., pp. 73–75.
15. Ibid., pp. 106–109, 113.
16. Stjepan Šiber, *Prevare, zablude, istina: ratni dnevnik 1992*, Rabić, Sarajevo, 2000, pp. 18–21.
17. See Sead Trhulj, *Mladi Muslimani*, Sarajevo, BBR, 1995.
18. See *Sarajevski proces – Suđenje muslimanskim intelektualcima 1983 g.: Sabrani dokumenti*, Bosanski institut, Zürich, 1987.
19. Alija Izetbegović, *Islamska Deklaracija*, 'Bosna', Sarajevo, 1990, p. 46.
20. Ibid., p. 37.
21. Alija Izetbegović, *Islam između istoka i zapada*, Svjetlost, Sarajevo, 1996.
22. Adil Zulfikarpašić, *The Bosniak*, Hurst and Co., London, 1998, p. 130.
23. Alija Izetbegović, *Sjećanja: Autobiografski zapis*, TKD Šahinpašić, Sarajevo, 2001, pp. 67–68.
24. Maid Hadžiomeragić, *Stranka Demokratske Akcije i stvarnost*, Unikopis, Sarajevo, 1991, pp. 75–77.
25. Ibid., p. 163.
26. Muhamed Borogovac, *Rat u Bosni i Hercegovini: Politički aspekti*, Zadarska tiskara, Zadar, 2000, p. 55.
27. Adil Zulfikarpašić, *Članci i intervjui povodom 70–godišnjice*, Bošnjački institut, Sarajevo, 1991, p. 326.
28. Borogovac, *Rat u Bosni i Hercegovini*, pp. 28–29.
29. Dževad Pašić, *Zemlja između istoka i zapada: Tuzla – odbrana kontinuiteta državnosti Bosne i Hercegovine*, Bosnia ARS, Tuzla, 1996, p. 223.
30. Hasan Čengić, interview in *Armija Bosne i Hercegovine 1992.-1995.*, NIPP 'Ljiljan', Sarajevo, 1997, pp. 124–125.
31. Hamid Bahto, interview in *Armija Bosne i Hercegovine*, p. 120.
32. Šefko Hodžić, *Bosanski ratnici*, DES, Sarajevo, 1998, p. 13.
33. Fikret Muslimović, *Odbrana Republike*, NIPP Ljiljan, Sarajevo, 1995, p. 206
34. Ibid., p. 206; 'Muslim Party Anniversary', BBC Summary of World Broadcasts, 19 July 1995, from *Oslobođenje*, 13–20 July 1995; Hodžić, *Bosanski ratnici*, p. 13.
35. Čengić, interview in *Armija Bosne i Hercegovine*, p. 125.
36. Hodžić, *Bosanski ratnici*, pp. 13–14.

37. Ibid., p. 18.
38. Sefer Halilović, speech at the promotion for his book *Lukava Strategija* held at the Army House in Sarajevo, 8 October 1997. Špegelj himself helped organise the defences of Posavina in northern Bosnia as an extension of Croatia's own defences against Serbia.
39. Hodžić, *Bosanski ratnici*, p. 18; Muslimović, *Odbrana Republike*, p. 207.
40. Hodžić, *Bosanski ratnici*, pp. 18–20.
41. Šefko Hodžić, 'Kako je nastajala Armija (6): junaci i stradalnici Podrinja', *Oslobođenje*, 21 April 1997, p. 15.
42. Kadijević, p. 93.
43. Smail Čekić, *Agresija na Bosnu i genocid nad Bošnjacima 1991–1993*, NIPP Ljiljan, Sarajevo, 1994, pp. 78–80.
44. Ratko Mladić, 'Izdaja u vrhovima', interview in *NIN*, 7 January 1994, pp. 55–57.
45. Ratko Mladić, 'Tragična konfuzija', interview in *NIN*, 14 January 1994, p. 54.
46. BBC Summary of World Broadcasts 4 July 1991, from Belgrade home service 1200 gmt 3 Jul 91.
47. BBC Summary of World Broadcasts 4 July 1991, from Yugoslav News Agency 1554 gmt 2 Jul 91.
48. Mladić, 'Izdaja u vrhovima', p. 57.
49. Laura Silber and Allan Little, *The Death of Yugoslavia*, Penguin, London, 1995, pp. 171–172.
50. Mladić, 'Tragična konfuzija', p. 55.
51. BBC Summary of World Broadcasts 12 March 1992, from Yugoslav News Agency 1123 gmt 10 Mar 92.
52. BBC Summary of World Broadcasts 12 October 1991, from Yugoslav News Agency 1640 gmt 8 Oct 91.
53. Snežana Trifunovska (ed.), *Yugoslavia through documents from its creation to its dissolution*, Martinus Nijhoff Publishers, Dordrecht, Boston and London, 1994, No. 134, pp. 412–413.
54. Borisav Jović, *Poslednji dani SFRJ*, Politika, Belgrade, 1996, p. 420.
55. Slobodan Srdanović, *Pale – Ratna hronika*, Svet Knjige, Belgrade, 1998, pp. 5–9.
56. Šiber, p. 20.
57. BBC Summary of World Broadcasts 13 December 1991, from Yugoslav News Agency 1900 gmt 10 Dec 91, Yugoslav News Agency 1624 gmt 11 Dec 91 and Croatian Radio 0905 gmt 12 Dec 91.
58. Jović, p. 421.

59. BBC Summary of World Broadcasts 3 December 1991, from Yugoslav News Agency 1445 gmt 29 Nov 91.
60. BBC Summary of World Broadcasts 1 January 1992, from Yugoslav News Agency 2252 gmt 30 Dec 91.
61. BBC Summary of World Broadcasts 3 December 1991, from Yugsoslav News Agency 1445 gmt 29 Nov 91.
62. Čekić., pp. 84, 169–170.
63. Ibid., pp. 80–81, 105–141.
64. Srdanović, pp. 19, 24–25.
65. Čekić, pp. 78–80.
66. Jović, pp. 430–431.
67. Ibid., p. 431.
68. BBC Summary of World Broadcasts 12 February 1992, from Yugoslav News Agency 1413 gmt 10 Feb 92
69. Ratko Mladić, 'Bio sam drzak', interview in *NIN*, 21 January 1994, p. 57.
70. Ratko Mladić, 'Parada lažnih spasitelja', interview in *NIN*, 28 January 1994, p. 55.
71. Ibid., p. 55.
72. Muharem Kržić, *Zločini nad banjalučkom krajinom '92–'94*, Muharem Kržić, Sarajevo, n.d., pp. 59, 102.
73. Jović, pp. 448–449.
74. Mladić, 'Parada lažnih spasitelja', pp. 55–56.
75. Jović, p. 452.
76. BBC Summary of World Broadcasts 12 May 1992, from Belgrade TV 1730 gmt 9 May 92.
77. Mladić, 'Parada lažnih spasitelja', p. 56.
78. *Službeni glasnik srpskog naroda u Bosni i Hercegovini*, 12–17 May 1992, p. 219; BBC Summary of World Broadcasts 14 May 1992, from Yugoslav News Agency 1901 gmt 12 May 92.
79. Mladić, 'Parada lažnih spasitelja', p. 56.
80. BBC Summary of World Broadcasts 21 May 1992, from Yugoslav News Agency 1849 gmt 19 May 92.
81. *Službeni glasnik srpskog naroda u Bosni i Hercegovini*, no. 4, 23 March 1992, p. 60.
82. BBC Summary of World Broadcasts 13 May 1992, from Radio Belgrade 2000 gmt 9 May 92.
83. Mladić, 'Parada lažnih spasitelja', p. 56.
84. Silber and Little, pp. 226–227.
85. Sefer Halilović, *Lukava Strategija*, Maršal d.o.o. PJ 'Matica Sandžaka', Sarajevo, 1997, pp. 55–56.

86. President Izetbegović's speech at meeting of the Congress of Bosnian Intellectuals, Office of the Army, Sarajevo, 29 November 1997.

87. Efendić, p. 108.

88. Silber and Little, pp. 247–248.

89. Munir Alibabić-Munja, *Bosna u Kandžama KOS-a*, Behar, Sarajevo, 1996, p. 46.

90. Efendić, pp. 109–110.

91. Halilović, *Lukava Strategija*, pp. 60–62; Marko Lopušina, *Ubij bližnjeg svog: Jugoslovenska tajna policija 1945/1995*, NIPTV Novosti DD, Belgrade, 1996, p. 243; Muslimović, *Odbrana Republike*, pp. 23–25; Silber and Little, pp. 262–263.

92. Silber and Little, p. 324.

93. Lopušina, p. 392.

94. Halilović, *Lukava Strategija*, p. 61; Alibabić, p. 45.

95. Alija Delimustafić, 'Pregovaraću do sudnjeg dana', interview in *NIN*, Belgrade, 20 December 1991.

96. Alibabić, pp. 37, 41–42, 50–51; Halilović, *Lukava Strategija*, p. 61.

97. Halilović, *Lukava Strategija*, pp. 64–65.

98. Alibabić, p. 50.

99. Efendić, pp. 244–248.

100. Đuro Kozar, 'Soldier without an Army and Homeland', AIM Sarajevo, 21 January 1999.

101. Hazim Begović, 'On the tail of events', interview in *Slobodna Bosna*, 19 November 1991.

102. Cvijetin Milivojević, 'Ready for war', *Borba*, 28 August 1991, p. 10.

103. 'Bosnian Minister accused of working with Croats', Tanjug, 1534 gmt 23 Sep 91.

104. BBC Summary of World Broadcasts 11 April 1992, from Tanjug 1758 gmt 9 Apr 92.

105. Efendić, p. 181.

106. Hodžić, 'Junaci i stradalnici Podrinja', p. 15.

107. Hodžić, *Bosanski ratnici*, p. 42.

108. Pašić, pp. 224–226.

109. Ibid., pp. 226–230.

110. Vahid Karavelić, interview in *Prva Linija*, no. 36, Year 4, 15 December 1995, p. 4.

111. Pašić, pp. 230–231.

112. Hodžić, *Bosanski ratnici*, p. 94.

113. Efendić, pp. 201–210.

114. Borogovac, *Rat u Bosni i Hercegovini*, pp. 59–60.

Chapter 2

1. Efendić, p. 80.
2. Silber and Little, pp. 248–253.
3. Efendić, p. 111; Šiber, pp. 34–35.
4. Efendić, pp. 112–113, 161–163.
5. Hodžić, *Bosanski ratnici*, p. 21.
6. Šiber, pp. 37–38.
7. Hodžić, *Bosanski ratnici*, pp. 23–24; Efendić, pp. 147–150; Šiber, pp. 39, 221–223.
8. The 'Croatian Armed Forces' sometimes also went by the name 'Croatian Defence Alliance', whose initials were also 'HOS'.
9. The Lisbon Agreement brokered by the EC in February 1992, which collapsed when Izetbegović pulled out of it, envisioned the division of Bosnia-Herzegovina into three ethnically defined parastates. See Silber and Little, pp. 241–242.
10. Efendić, pp. 122–124.
11. Rasim Hodžić and Šefik Sabljica (eds), *Zbirka propisa iz odbrane*, Studenska Štamparija Univerzitet Sarajevo, 1995, p. 51.
12. Ibid., p. 58.
13. *Pravila oružanih snaga*, Glavni štab oružanih snaga Republike Bosne i Hercegovine, Sarajevo, 1992, p. 405.
14. Ibid., p. 241.
15. Ibid., pp. 237–238.
16. Sefer Halilović, 'U svojoj sljedećoj knjizi dokazat ću da je Alija Izetbegović, koji se javno zalagao za cjelovitu Bosnu, poduzeo sve da je podijeli !', interview in *Globus*, no. 360, 31 October 1997, p. 24; Jovan Divjak, 'Izetbegović me pitao otkud znam za akciju na Špicastoj Stijeni !', interview in *Slobodna Bosna*, no. 36, 12 January 1997, p. 15.
17. Divjak, 'Izetbegović me pitao … ', p. 15.
18. Mirko Pejanović, *Bosansko pitanje i Srbi u Bosni i Hercegovini*, Bosanska knjiga, Sarajevo, 1999, p. 96.
19. Ibid., pp. 101–102.
20. Ibid., p. 97; Mustafa Hajrulahović, interview in *East European Reporter*, July-August 1992.
21. Efendić, p. 162.
22. Ibid., pp. 143–144.
23. Ibid., pp. 190–201.
24. Hodžić, *Bosanski ratnici*, pp. 27–28.
25. Muslimović, *Odbrana Republike*, p. 209.
26. Efendić, p. 131.

27. Hodžić, *Bosanski ratnici*, p. 50.
28. Efendić, pp. 171–178.
29. Šefko Hodžić, 'Kako je nastajala Armija (5): Stvaranje legendi', *Oslobođenje*, 20 April 1997, p. 12.
30. Halilović, *Lukava strategija*, pp. 60–62.
31. Pejanović, pp. 99–100.
32. Šiber, p. 95.
33. Efendić, pp. 314–316.
34. Pejanović, p. 100.
35. Alija Izetbegovic, interview in *Armija Bosne i Hercegovine*, p. 8.
36. Marko Attila Hoare, 'Bosnian Serbs and Anti-Bosnian Serbs', *Bosnia Report*, New Series no. 8, January-February 1999.
37. Hodžić, *Bosanski ratnici*, p. 38; Efendić, pp. 127–129.
38. BBC Summary of World Reports, 28 April 1992, from Tanjug, 26 April 1992.
39. Halilović, *Lukava strategija*, pp. 57–58.
40. Ibid., pp. 58–59; Hodžić, *Bosanski ratnici*, pp. 32–34; Efendić, pp. 319–321.
41. Efendić, p. 129.
42. Jovan Divjak, 'The first phase, 1992–1993: Struggle for survival and genesis of the Army of Bosnia-Herzegovina', in Branka Magaš and Ivo Žanić, *The war in Croatia and Bosnia-Herzegovina 1991–1995*, Frank Cass, London, 2001, p. 157.
43. Hodžić, *Bosanski ratnici*, p. 30.
44. Fahira Fejzić, 'Koze, knezi i knjazovi', *Ljiljan*, no. 204, 11 December 1996, pp. 17–18.
45. Hodžić, *Bosanski ratnici*, pp. 28–29.
46. Halilović, *Lukava strategija*, pp. 32–33.
47. Hodžić, *Bosanski ratnici*, p. 29.
48. Vladislav Pogarčić, *Why was the Croatian Community of Herzeg-Bosnia created?*, Republic of Bosnia-Herzegovina – Croatian Community of Herzeg-Bosnia, Office of the President, 26 July 1993, p. 3; 'Ko to hoće trgovati Dudakovićem?', *Dani*, no. 113, 30 July 1999.
49. Hodžić, *Bosanski ratnici*, p. 49.
50. Muslimović, *Odbrana Republike*, pp. 101, 166–167.
51. Fikret Muslimović, interview in *Armija Bosne i Hercegovine*, pp. 110–111.
52. Divjak, 'The first phase, 1992–1993', p. 161.
53. Marko Marković and Marko Jurić, 'Bitka na Kupreškoj visoravni', in *Globus*, 17 April 1992.

54. See Davor Butković, 'Pogled u Bosnu', in *Globus*, 22 November 1991.

55. Zoran Daskalović, 'Vitezovi opskurnoga stola', *Feral Tribune*, 13 October 1997, p. 5.

56. Soldiers working at the ARBiH's outfitting shop in Tuzla told this author in August 1995 that Tuzla Serbs still frequently enlisted in the HVO in preference to the ARBiH, since the pay was better.

57. Fuad Kovač, 'U konacima Mehmeda Fatiha rođeni su hrvatski zločinci Rajić i Blaškić', *Ljiljan*, no. 185, 31 July 1996, p. 28.

58. Mate Bašić and Marko Barišić, 'Operacija 'Trojanski Konj''', in *Globus*, 17 April 1992.

59. On the strategic importance of Kupres, see 'U Pakao kroz Kupreška vrata', in *Globus*, 10 April 1992.

60. Ismet Hadžiosmanović, 'Devetog maja 1993. nazvao sam Izetbegovića i rekao mu: 'Haram ti bilo, Alija !', interview in *Slobodna Bosna*, no. 19, 19 May 1996, p. 11.

61. Iko Stanić, 'Ako nas je Tuđman izdao, Izetbegović nije smio !', interview in *Slobodna Bosna*, no. 8, 15 December 1995, pp. 6–7.

62. Silber and Little, p. 324.

63. Efendić, p. 110.

64. Ibid., p. 120.

65. Ibid., pp. 135–136, 229–230; Šefko Hodžić, 'Kako je nastajala Armija (11): Gdje je Hrvatsko Vijeće Odbrane?', *Oslobođenje*, 26 April 1992, p. 21.

66. Halilović, *Lukava Strategija*, p. 62.

67. Fejzović, 'Koze, knezi i knjazovi', p. 19; Nedžad Latić, 'Svjedoci tvrde da ljudi Nasera Orića stoje iza 19 atentat u Srebrenici', *Ljiljan*, no. 186, 7 August 1996, pp. 19–20.

68. 'Bosnian newspaper editor accuses Tuzla authorities over fall of Cerska', BBC Summary of World Broadcasts, 8 March 1993, from Radio Bosnia-Herzegovina, 5 March 1993.

69. Mustafa Hajrulahović, interview in *East European Reporter*, July-August 1992.

70. Sefer Halilović, interview in *Armija Bosne i Hercegovine*, p. 14.

71. Vanessa Vasić-Janeković, 'Croatian Forces Play Insidious Game', in *War Report*, September 1992.

72. Sefer Halilović, 'Savjest mi je mirna, Hrvatima sam pomagao koliko sam mogao', interview in *Panorama*, 21 June 1995, p. 9; Šiber, pp. 111–122.

73. Šefko Hodžić, *Vitezovi i huni*, Sarajevo, OKO, 1996, p. 67.

74. Lopušina, p. 236.

75. Pašić, pp. 163–164.

76. Srdanović, pp. 12–13.

77. Alibabić, p. 48.

78. Hodžić, *Bosanski ratnici*, p. 39.

79. Davor Domazet-Lošo, 'Uloga JNA kao srpske imperijalne sile u bosanskohercegovačkom ratu', *Hrvatski Vojnik*, February 1998, p. 7.

80. Vojislav Šešelj, interview in *South Slav Journal*, vol. 16, no. 3–4 (61–62) Autumn-Winter 1995, pp. 82–85.

81. Hadžija Hadžiabdić, 'Doboj – ključ ka integraciji BiH', *Prva Linija*, no. 54, year 4, September 1997, p. 34.

82. Bašić and Barišić, 'Operacija Trojanski Konj'.

83. *Strategija opštenarodne odbrane i društvene samozaštite SFRJ*, Savezni sekretarijat za narodnu odbranu, Belgrade, 1987, pp. 89–90.

84. Ibid., p. 94.

85. Ibid., p. 113.

86. Hodžić, *Bosanski ratnici*, p. 29.

87. Šefko Hodžić, 'Kako je nastajala Armija (12): Sarajevo 2. maja '92', *Oslobođenje*, 17 April 1997.

88. Silber and Little, pp. 262–263; Alibabić, pp. 62–63.

89. Silber and Little, pp. 263–267.

90. Efendić, p. 266.

91. 'Izetbegović on offer to JNA pays tribute to citizens' defence of republic' BBC Summary of World Broadcasts, 15 May 1992, from Radio Bosnia-Herzegovina, 13 May 1992; 'Bosnia-Herzegovina Territorial Defence review security situation', BBC Summary of World Broadcasts, 18 May 1992, from Radio Bosnia-Herzegovina, 15 May 1992.

92. Vahid Karavelić, 'Tako se branilo Sarajevo', *Prva Linija*, no. 21, p. 8; Nusret Hodžić, 'Glava je spašena', *Prva Linija*, no. 42, pp. 12–13.

93. Pašić, pp. 289–318.

94. Šefko Hodžić, 'Žuč kao sudbina', *Prva Linija*, no. 53, pp. 24–26.

95. Divjak, 'The first phase, 1992–1993', pp. 162–165.

96. Alibabić, p. 64; Halilović, *Lukava strategija*, p. 10.

97. Hodžić, *Bosanski ratnici*, p. 40; Efendić, p. 230.

98. Mark Heinrich, 'Serbs gloated as warlord bloodbath swept Sarajevo', *Reuter Library Report*, 8 November 1993.

99. Mustafa Hajrulahović Talijan, 'Igman je naša najružna ratna priča', *Ljiljan*, 18 March 1998, pp. 28–29.

100. Ibid., pp. 28–29; Zulfikar Ališpago Zuka, 'Nisam bio kralj Igmana, već borac koji je pobijedio neprijatelja u 54 bitke', interview in *Ljiljan*, no. 204, 11 December 1996, pp. 21–23.

101. Vildana Selimbegović, 'Jusuf Juka Prazina: Vuk ili Kojot', *Dani*, no. 55, May 1997, pp. 38–41; Vildana Selimbegović, 'Želio sam da ubijem Juku', *Dani*, no. 58, August 1997, pp. 46–47; Ališpago, op. cit.

102. Hodžić, *Bosanski ratnici*, p. 134; Hajrulahović, op. cit.

103. Esad Hećimović, 'Kako su prodali Srebrenicu i sačuvali vlast', *Dani*, specijalno izdanje, September 1998, p. 28.

104. These included the KOS agent Sead Rekić, an ally of Muslimović and Alispahić. Alibabić, pp. 71–77; Hajrulahović, 'Igman je naša najružna ratna priča', pp. 28–29; Zulfikar Ališpago Zuka, deputy commander of the 6th Corps, attributes the fall of the key point of Golo brdo to the treason of a Serb platoon. See Zulfikar Ališpago Zuka, 'Nikad niko nije želio izvesti vojni udar u Sarajevo, već odstraniti narodne komandante iz Armije BiH', *Ljiljan*, no. 205, 18 December 1996, p. 23.

105. International Criminal Tribunal for the former Yugoslavia, indictment of Zejnil Delalić, Zdravko Mučić, Hazim Delić and Esad Landžo, 19 March 1996. Mučić, Delić and Landžo were convicted and sentenced to prison terms in 1998.

106. Momčilo Mitrović, *Muslimanski logor Visoko, 1992–1993 (Dnevnik i kazivanja logoraša)*, 2nd ed., Vojska, Belgrade, 1995.

107. International Criminal Tribunal for the former Yugoslavia, indictment of Naser Orić, 28 March 2003.

108. 'Murderer from Srebrenica', *Reporter*, Banja Luka, 10 April 2001.

109. Pejanović, pp. 102–104.

110. Hodžić, *Bosanski ratnici*, pp. 51–53; Efendić, pp. 230, 300–304.

111. Efendić, pp. 307–313.

112. Šefko Hodžić, 'Kako je nastajala Armija (17): Prve brigade', *Oslobođenje*, 3 May 1997, p. 21.

113. Hodžić, *Bosanski ratnici*, pp. 62–64.

114. Ibid., p. 60.

115. Halilović, *Lukava strategija*, pp. 139–141.

116. Hodžić, *Bosanski ratnici*, p. 99.

117. Alibabić, p. 47.

118. 'Serbian member of Bosnian Presidency gives reasons for resignation', BBC Summary of World Broadcasts, 27 August 1992, from Tanjug, 24 August 1992.

119. Šiber, p. 46.

Chapter 3

1. Hodžić, 'Gdje je Hrvatsko vijeće odbrane?', p. 21.
2. *Globus*, 3 September 1993; Dario Brkić and Dijana Krešić, 'Prostorom zapadne Hercegovine vladaju udbaške obitelji Stojić, Bradvica, Boban, Ćorić,', *Slobodna Bosna*, 7 September 1997, pp. 15–17; 'Federalna politika i hrvatski elementi odgovorni za subverzivne aktivnosti u jugozapadnoj Hercegovini', report by OSCE Mission to Bosnia-Herzegovina Regional Centre Mostar, reproduced in *Dani*, br. 59, September 1997, pp. 47–61; Miljenko Jergović, 'Mate Boban 1940–1997: Karadžić's 'brother in Christ'', *Bosnia Report*, Issue 19, June-July-August 1997, pp. 13–14.
3. Alibabić, p. 44.
4. Jergović, op. cit.
5. Sefer Halilović, interview in *Nacional*, br. 102, p. 13.
6. 'Federalna politika i hrvatski elementi', p. 55.
7. Jasna Babić, 'U Samoboru je 14. kolovoza uhićen Pero Skopljak, Bosanski Hrvat optužen za ratne zločine: bit će izručen haškom sudu da bi se zaštitili Dario Kordić i Ivica Rajić', *Nacional*, br. 92, 20 August 1997, p. 4.
8. Kovać, 'U konacima Mehmeda Fatiha rođeni su hrvatski zločinci Rajić i Blaškić', p. 28.
9. Sefer Halilović, interview in *Armija Bosne i Hercegovine*, p. 14.
10. Tarik Kulenović, 'Pripreme za rat i početak rata u Bosni i Hercegovini 1992. godine', in *Polemos*, vol. 1, no. 1, January-June 1998; Šiber, pp. 47, 53.
11. 'Croat paramilitary HOS unit takes the oath in Čapljina', BBC Summary of World Broadcasts, 21 July 1992, from Radio Bosnia-Herzegovina, Sarajevo 2000 gmt 19 Jul 92.
12. Dobroslav Paraga, interview in *Slobodna Bosna*, 24 August 1997, pp. 11–12.
13. Attila Hoare, 'The Croatian Project to Partition Bosnia-Herzegovina', *East European Quarterly*, XXXI, no. 1, March 1997, p. 128.
14. Davor Butković, 'U Derventi je izveden puč !', in *Globus*, 24 June 1992; interview with Armin Pohara, *Globus* 31 July 1992.
15. Vlado Vurušić, 'Boj zmajeva i Belih Orlova', in *Globus*, 3 April 1992.
16. Anton Tus, interview in *Tjednik*, 1 August 1997, p. 24; Martin Špegelj,'Rat završava na koridoru', *BiH Eksklusiv*, 16 June 1995, p. 3.
17. Špegelj, 'Rat završava na koridoru', p. 3.

18. 'Civilians flee last non-Serb enclave on Sava River', *Reuters Library Report*, 8 October 1992.
19. 'Fighting in and around Jajce continues', *Reuters Library Report*, 31 October 1992.
20. Hodžić, *Bosanski ratnici*, pp. 189–191.
21. Roman Majetić, 'Prozor je razbijen !', in *Globus*, 30 October 1992.
22. Pogarčić, p. 6.
23. Ante Prkačin, interview in *Globus*, 7 May 1993.
24. Ante Prkačin, interview in *Globus*, 9 July 1993.
25. Džemaludin Latić, interview in *Globus*, 30 June 1993.
26. Milivoj Petković, Interview in *Slobodna Dalmacija*, 26 February 1993.
27. Sefer Halilović, interview in *Armija Bosne i Hercegovine*, pp. 26–27.
28. Hoare, 'The Croatian Project to Partition Bosnia-Herzegovina', pp. 132–133.
29. Božo Raić, Interview in *Globus*, 22 January 1993.
30. Roman Majetić, 'Komandosi iz Čapljine još ratuju s turcima', in *Globus*, 23 April 1993.
31. Musadik Borogovac, 'Na Izetbegovićev zahtjev Hasan Čengić je za dva sata napisao prijedlog ustava islamske BiH !', interview in *Slobodna Bosna*, 16 October 1999, pp. 37–39.
32. Borogovac, *Rat u Bosni i Hercegovini*, pp. 87–88.
33. 'Fighting goes on in Bosanski Brod; Presidency delegation holds talks there', BBC Summary of World Broadcasts, 30 March 1992, from Radio Bosnia-Herzegovina, Sarajevo 0830 gmt 14 Mar 93.
34. 'Bosnian Muslim commander arrested in Tuzla', BBC Summary of World Broadcasts, 16 March 93
35. Borogovac, *Rat u Bosni i Hercegovini*, pp. 70–71.
36. 'Senior Bosnian military figure resigns, accusing Army HQ of high treason', BBC Summary of World Broadcasts, 20 March 1993, from Croatian TV satellite service, Zagreb 1830 gmt 18 March 1993.
37. 'Fikret Abdić asks Mostar, Zagreb Muslims to join Bosnian Presidency delegation', BBC Summary of World Broadcasts, 5 August 1993, from Croatian Radio, Zagreb 1300 gmt 3 Aug 93.
38. Pašić, p. 224.
39. Safet Zajko, 'Čestitke u rovovima na Žuči', interview in *Armija Bosne i Hercegovine*, p. 25.
40. Rasim Imamović, interview in *Armija Bosne i Hercegovine*, p. 45.
41. Muslimović, *Odbrana Republike*, pp. 17, 49.
42. Ibid., pp. 13–16.
43. Ibid., pp. 30–32.
44. Alibabić, pp. 40–41; Halilović, *Lukava Strategija*, p. 77.
45. Muslimović, *Odbrana Republike*, p. 20.

46. Halilović, *Lukava Strategija*, p. 72; Alibabić, pp. 48–49.
47. Halilović, *Lukava Strategija*, pp. 74–76.
48. Ibid., p. 76. Muslimović and Mujezinović, under the command of Vasiljević, had engaged in the monitoring and arrest of Albanian dissidents in Kosova during the 1980s (Medina Delalić and Jelena Stamenković, 'Kako je stvarana OVK', *Slobodna Bosna*, no. 90, 8 August 1998, p. 17).
49. Alibabić, pp. 89–90.
50. Efendić, p. 150.
51. Hodžić, *Bosanski ratnici*, pp. 134–135.
52. Ališpago, 'Nikad niko nije … ', pp. 23–24.
53. Pejanović, pp. 106–108.
54. Halilović, *Lukava Strategija*, pp. 105–108.
55. Ibid., p. 10.
56. Divjak, 'Izetbegović me pitao … ', p. 15.
57. Among these others, however, Lučarević includes Mahmutćehajić and Alibabić, themselves bitter critics of Izetbegović and Muslimović respectively. See Kerim Lučarević, interview in *Dani*, br. 64, 8 December 1997, pp. 9–11.
58. Hodžić, *Bosanski ratnici*, pp. 135–136.
59. Izetbegović, *Sjećanja*, pp. 153–154.
60. Ibid., p. 153.
61. Medina Delalić and Jelena Stamenković, 'Kako je Izetbegović štitio kriminal i zločin(c)e', *Slobodna Bosna*, no. 95, 10 September 1998, p. 6.
62. Ibid., p. 6; Halilović, *Lukava Strategija*, pp. 14–16.
63. Halilović, *Lukava Strategija*, pp. 29–38.
64. Ibid., p. 33.
65. Ibid., p. 35.
66. Hodžić, *Bosanski ratnici*, p. 138.
67. Sefer Halilović, 'Samo su trezoraši gori od podrumaša !', interview in *Slobodna Bosna*, no. 47, p. 11.
68. 'Ko (u) Visoko leti nisko (ne)pada)', *Slobodna Bosna*, no. 30, 20 October 1996, pp. 14–16.
69. *The ethnic cleansing of Croats in Bosnia and Herzegovina 1991–1993*, Office of the President of the Croatian Community of Herzeg-Bosna, Mostar, August 1993, p. 10.
70. Ivica Radoš, 'U ljeto i jesen 1993. vojnici Armije BiH pogubili su desetke civila u većinski hrvatskim selima Doljani, Uzdol i Grabovića: Samo na Stipica poljani iznad Doljana pogubili su 18

ljudi i na tom mjestu, natopljenom krvlju, ni danas ne raste trava', *Nacional*, no. 101, 22 October 1997, pp. 46–48.

71. One year after the creation of the King Tvrtko Brigade from the Sarajevan HVO, General Karavelić of the 1st Corps would accuse its soldiers of refusal to resist Serb attacks. See Vahid Karavelić, interview in *Armija Bosne i Hercegovine*, p. 86.

72. Ed Vulliamy, 'Croats who supped with the devil', *The Guardian*, 18 March 1996, p. 8.

73. Željko Rogošić, 'Šesti Korpus Armije BiH započeo strategijsko opkoljavanje Mostara !', in *Globus*, 9 July 1993; report by the Globus military staff 'Bugojno je palo: HVO je izgubio rat za Bosnu?', in *Globus*, 30 July 1993.

74. Chuck Sudetic, 'Killings in Bosnian Monastery Widen Croat-Muslim Divide', *The New York Times*, 31 December 1993.

75. Anto Pejčinović, 'Istina o Varešu', in *Nacional*, 18 August 1999; Jasna Babić, 'Pokolj u Stupnom Dolu i rat u Varešu planirali su Hrvatski ekstremisti u dogovoru sa Srbima !', in *Globus*, 12 November 1993; Natasha Narayan, report in *The Guardian*, 5 November 1993.

76. Rusmir Mahmutćehajić, *Čitanje historije i povjerenje u Bosni: Kriva politika*, Radio Kameleon Tuzla, Tuzla, 1998, p. 67.

77. Ibid, p. 67.

78. Adnan Jahić, 'Krijeposna muslimanska država', in *Zmaj od Bosne*, no. 51, 17 September 1993, reproduced in *Front Slobode*, Tuzla, 23 August 1996.

79. According to Senad Pećanin and Vildana Selimbegović, 'Istina o Cacinim zločinima', *Dani*, no. 62, 10 November 1997, pp. 16–20. *Ljiljan's* investigative team, however, concludes that Topalović did not victimise Serbs or Croats but rather those with material possessions worth appropriating, and that he was motivated by psychopathological sadism rather than racism. See 'Caco se osiguravao tako što je od svjedoka pravio saučesnike', *Ljiljan*, no. 254, 26 November 1997, pp. 18–19.

80. Hajrulahović, 'Igman je naša najružna ratna priča'. Halilović however claimed that Topalović had been appointed and approved as commander of the 10th Brigade by none other than Hajrulahović, on the grounds of his popularity and influence in Sarajevo. See Halilović, interview in *Panorama*, p. 8.

81. Senad Pećanin and Vildana Selimbegović, 'Kako je ubijen Caco', *Dani*, no. 64, 8 December 1997; Alibabić, pp. 75–76.

82. Munib Bišić, 'Halilović je pismeno tražio ukidanje Ministarstva Odbrane da bi i MUP stavio pod svoju kontrolu – iza toga se krila

ambicija da postane vladar svih naših sudbina', *Ljiljan*, no. 19 November 1997, pp. 26–27. Bišić gave the figure of 948 disarmed policemen.

83. Izetbegović, *Sjećanja*, p. 154.

84. Delalić and Stamenković, 'Kako je Izetbegović štitio kriminal i zločin(c)e', p. 9.

85. Izetbegović, *Sjećanja*, p. 155.

86. Pećanin and Selimbegović, 'Kako je ubijen Caco'; Izetbegović, *Sjećanja*, pp. 155–156.

87. Delalić and Stamenković, 'Kako je Izetbegović štitio kriminal i zločin(c)e', p. 9.

88. 'First corps army takes over control of Bosnian Croat HVO unit in Sarajevo', BBC Summary of World Broadcasts, 8 November 1993, from Radio Bosnia-Herzegovina, 6 November 1993.

89. 'Sarajevo Croats tell Muslims to stop aggression or UN must organise evacuation', BBC Summary of World Broadcasts, 12 November 1993, from Croatian Radio, 10 November 1993.

90. Izetbegović, *Sjećanja*, p. 157.

91. Sejo Omeragić, 'Bosno moja, ispod 'Trebevića'', *Slobodna Bosna*, no. 10, 12 January 1996, pp. 15–17.

92. Murat Kahrović, *Seferovo ratno doba*, OKO, Sarajevo, 2002, pp. 173–176.

93. Pejanović, p. 100.

94. Dragan Vikić, 'Zaboravljeni komandant iz pjesme i legende', interview in *Ljiljan*, no. 220, 2 April 1997, p. 12.

95. Alibabić himself apparently sent detailed reports of the activities of Muslim and other paramilitary formations to the Ministry of the Interior in Belgrade up until the start of the war. See Mirsad Sinanović and Mustafa Borović, 'Munir Alibabić je izvještaje o Zelenim Beretkama slao u Beograd, a za taj posao primao deviznu plaću u Delimustafićevom moniku', *Ljiljan*, no.177a, 5 June 1996, pp. 8–9.

Chapter 4

1. Muslimović, *Odbrana Republike*, p. 199.

2. Ibid., p. 203.

3. Fikret Muslimović, 'Strategijski aspekti odbrane RBiH', in *Moralni aspekti odbrane*, Press Centar Armija RBiH, Sarajevo, January 1995, p. 6.

4. Ibid., pp. 9–10.

5. Ibid., pp. 12–13.

6. Halilović, *Lukava Strategija*, pp. 32, 36.

7. *Oslobođenje*, 13 May 1996; Nedžad Latić, 'Agenti nisu htjeli ubiti Fikreta Abdića nego Fikreta Muslimovića', *Ljiljan*, no. 171, 24 April 1996, p. 9.

8. *Priručnik za komandira odjeljenja (prvo izdanje)*, Štab vrhovne komande oružanih snaga RBiH Uprava za obuku, školstvo, pravila i propise, Travnik, 1994, pp. 3–4.

9. Ibid., p. 5.

10. Rasim Delić, *Army – Key to the Peace*, Press Centre of the Army of the Republic of Bosnia and Herzegovina, August 1994, p. 8.

11. Rasim Delić, interview in *Armija Bosne i Hercegovine*, p. 64.

12. Rasim Delić, interview in *Armija Bosne i Hercegovine*, pp. 42–43.

13. Rašid Muminović, 'Uloga Islamske zajednice na ostvarivanju vjerskih potreba pripadnika ARBiH', *Duhovna snaga odbrane*, Press Centre of the Army of the Republic of Bosnia-Herzegovina, Sarajevo, February 1994, p. 86.

14. Fikret Muslimović, 'Uloga komandovanja i rukovođenja u ostvarivanju vjerskih potreba pripadnika Armije RBiH', *Duhovna snaga odbrane*, pp. 87–94.

15. Ibid., p. 93.

16. Govor prof. dr Mustafa eff. Ćerića, reisu-l-ulleme Islamske zajednice u Republici Bosni i Hercegovini na Seminaru 'Uloga vjere u razvijanju patriotskog jedinstva odbrambeno-oslobodilačkih snaga' – Sarajevo, 31. januara 1994. godine, *Duhovna snaga odbrane*, p. 9.

17. Ibid., pp. 13–14.

18. See Nedžad Latić, 'Hej, hej, nek se znade, postojale Muslimanske brigade', *Ljiljan*, no. 273, p. 10.

19. Munir Gavrankapetanović, *Poruka borcu – ranjenom oboljelom amputircu*, Uprava za politička pitanja Armije RBiH, Sarajevo, July 1996.

20. Interview with Halil Brzina, in *Armija Bosne i Hercegovina*, p. 66.

21. Ibid., p. 67.

22. Asim Koričić, interview in *Armija Bosne i Hercegovine*, p. 70.

23. Ibid., p. 72.

24. Chuck Sudetich, 'Crni Labudovi', *BiH Eksklusiv*, 30 June 1995, no. 140, p. 3.

25. Vildana Selimbegović, 'Kako je nestajala Armija BiH: Pojela je politika', *Dani*, no. 54, April 1997, pp. 24–25.

26. Framework Agreement establishing a Federation in the areas of the Republic of Bosnia and Herzegovina with a majority Bosniak and Croat population, and Outline of a Preliminary Agreement for a Confederation between the Republic of Croatia and the Federation, 2 March 1994.

27. Željko Grubešić, 'Godina jačanja ugleda Armije RBiH', *Prva Linija*, no. 19, year 3, December 1994, pp. 24–25.

28. Rasim Delić, *Bosnia is Here*, Press Centre of the Army of the Republic of Bosnia and Herzegovina, Sarajevo, October 1995, p. 8.

29. Sead Delić, interview in *Armija Bosne i Hercegovine*, p. 92.

30. Hazim Šadić, interview in *Armija Bosne i Hercegovine*, p. 74.

31. 'HVO rejects government claim to control of forces in northern Bosnia', BBC Summary of World Broadcasts, 19 December 1994, from Croatian Radio Herzeg-Bosna, 16 December 1994.

32. Haris Halilović, 'Efikasnijim komandovanjem do slobode', *Prva Linija*, br. 20, year 4, January 1995, p. 4.

33. Delić, *Bosnia is here*, pp. 74–75.

34. Šadić, interview in *Armija Bosne i Hercegovine*, p. 74.

35. 'Anti-Karadžić Serbs form unit within Bosnian Army', BBC Summary of World Broadcasts, 26 July 1994, from Radio Bosnia-Herzegovina, 22 July 1994; 'Serb battalion in Bosnian Army to include other nationalities', BBC Summary of World Broadcasts, 27 July 1994, from Radio Bosnia-Herzegovina, 25 July 1994.

36. Pejanović, pp. 97–98.

37. 224. Fejzović, 'Koze, knezi i knjazovi', p. 19; Latić, 'Svjedoci tvrde …', pp. 19–20.

38. 'Autonomy movement said to be growing in Tuzla region', BBC Summary of World Broadcasts, 13 October 1993, from Yugoslav Telegraph Service news agency, Belgrade, 11 October 1993.

39. Sead Delić, interview in *Armija Bosne i Hercegovine*, p. 93.

40. Hećimović, p. 27.

41. Ibid., p. 50.

42. Ibid., pp. 51–52.

43. Ibid., p. 52.

44. Pejanović, pp. 110–111.

45. Hećimović, pp. 39–40.

46. *The Military Balance 1994–1995*, International Institute for Strategic Studies, London, 1994, pp. 82–83.

47. Mustafa Borović, 'Tunel', *Ljiljan*, no. 186, 7 August 1996, p. 5.

48. Divjak, 'The first phase, 1992–1993', pp. 165–166.

49. *The Military Balance 1994–1995*, pp. 84–85.

50. Jovan Divjak, interview in *Armija Bosne i Hercegovine*, p. 96.

51. Norman Cigar, *The Right to Defence: Thoughts on the Bosnian Arms Embargo*, Institute for European Defence and Strategic Studies, London, 1995; Martin Špegelj, 'The War in ex-Yugoslavia and its Resolution', Zagreb, 1995 (English translation of unpublished text).

52. Srdanović, pp. 54–57.

53. 'Government briefed on Serb military activities in eastern Bosnia', BBC Summary of World Broadcasts, 8 November 1994.

54. Paul Williams and Norman Cigar, *A Prima Facie Case for the Indictment of Slobodan Milosević*, Alliance to Defend Bosnia-Herzegovina, London, 1996, p. 11.

55. Halilović, *Lukava strategija*, pp. 89–100. Halilović claims that Čengić, as finance minister, refused to provide funds for the Army prior to the war's outbreak, insisting that soldiers themselves pay for their weapons.

56. Robert Fox, 'Islamic indoctrination of army splits Bosnian leadership', *The Daily Telegraph*, 6 February 1995.

57. James Risen and Doyle McManus, 'Clinton OK'd Arms Pipeline', *Los Angeles Times*, 5 April 1996.

58. See Sakib Mahmuljin, 'Više im nikada neće naumpasti da ovako krenu na nas !', interview in *Ljiljan*, no. 148, 15 November 1995, pp. 5–6.

59. Zemka Seferagić, 'Krajiški bedem Bosne', *Prva Linija*, November 1997, p. 20; Ramiz Dreković, interview in *Prva Linija*, 15 November 1995, p. 4; Izet Nanić, interview in *Armija Bosne i Hercegovine*, p. 104.

60. Salko Begić, 'Hrvatskoj smo skupo platili sve sto je učinila za Krajinu, a Jurlina je bio obični turista', interview in *Ljiljan*, 2 July 1997, pp. 22–23.

61. BBC Summary of World Broadcasts, 23 October 1993, from Croatian Radio, 22 October 1993.

62. 'Krajina Serbs providing military aid for Abdić', BBC Summary of World Broadcasts, 8 November 1993, from Radio Bosnia-Herzegovina, 5 November 1993.

63. Dreković, interview in *Armija Bosne i Hercegovine*, p. 7.

64. Interview with Hamdija Abdić, in *Armija Bosne i Hercegovine*, pp. 114–115; Samira Džanić, 'Povodom trogodišnjice operacije: 'Tigar – Sloboda 94'', *Prva Linija*, no. 53, July 1997, pp. 20–21.

65. *BBC World Service*, reports of 15 and 21 September 1994.

66. 'Bosnian Army commander reports major victory over Serb forces in Western Bosnia', BBC Radio, 27 October 1994, from Radio Bosnia-Herzegovina, 25 October 1994.

67. 'Muslim units capture two Serb strongholds near Bihać', BBC Radio, 31 October 1994, from Radio Bosnia-Herzegovina, 29 October 1994.

68. 'HVO forces in Bihać complain about lack of media attention', BBC Summary of World Broadcasts, 15 December 1994, from Croatian Radio, Zagreb, 1400 gmt 13 Dec 94.

69. See Attila Hoare, 'A rope supports a man who is hanged: NATO air-strikes and the end of Bosnian resistance', *East European Politics and Societies*, vol. 12, no. 2, spring 1998, pp. 203–221.

70. Hećimović, p. 27.

71. Nedžad Latić and Zehrudin Isaković, *Ratna sjećanja Mehmeda Alagića: Rat u Srednjoj Bosni*, Bemust, Zenica, 1997, p. 37.

72. Ibid., p. 49.

73. Hećimović, pp. 54–59.

74. Latić and Isaković, p. 65.

75. Hećimović, p. 58.

76. Vulliamy, op. cit.

77. Hećimović., pp. 74–82.

78. Ibid., pp. 45–46.

79. Mehmed Pargan, 'Baljkovića – najveći poraz Armije BiH', *Slobodna Bosna*, no. 88, pp. 28–30; Ismet Hasanović and Nirzad Karamujić, 'Lovačka puška bila je razlog da se Bošnjačko selo opkoli sa 12 transportera UN-a', interview in *Ljiljan*, no. 211, 29 January 1997, pp. 32–33.

80. Hećimović, pp. 9–13.

81. Ibid., pp. 61–71.

82. David Rohde, *A Safe Area – Srebrenica: Europe's Worst Massacre Since the Second World War*, Pocket Books, London, 1997, pp. 356–358.

83. Hećimović, p. 52.

84. Ibid., p. 59.

85. Mahmuljin, 'Više im nikada …', p. 6.

86. Hećimović., pp. 61–64.

87. Ibid., p. 69.

88. Ibid., p. 65.

89. Ibran Mustafić, 'Predsjedništvo i Generalštab su žrtvovali Srebrenicu !', *Slobodna Bosna*, no. 23, 14 July 1996, p. 6.

90. 'Pismo Generala Delića pripadnicima Armije', reproduced in *Slobodna Bosna*, no. 1, 4 September 1995, p. 17.

91. 'Tako je govorio Muslimović', *Slobodna Bosna*, no. 2, 21 September 1995, p.25.

92. 'The Split Declaration', reproduced in *Bosnia Report*, no. 11, June-August 1995, p. 5.

93. See Suad Arnautović, *Kako se branila Bosna: Vojno-politički eseji i komentari*, Promokult, Sarajevo, 1997, pp. 175–176.

94. Ronald Fogleman, Letter to the Editor, *Wall Street Journal*, 11 October 1995.

95. Hoare, 'A rope supports a man who is hanged', pp. 214–216.

96. Jane Perlez, 'Banja Luka: Not a target of assaults, yet beaten', *New York Times*, 2 November 1995; Anthony Loyd, 'Tigers ignore truce in fierce battle for land', *Times Newspapers Ltd*, 16 October 1995.

97. 'Attack on Banja Luka due soon: Bosnian commander', *Agence France Presse*, 23 September 1995; 'Bosnian liberation the only peace plan: Silajdžić', *Agence France Presse*, 24 September 1995.

98. Quoted in Branka Magaš, 'The tide of war turns in Bosnia-Herzegovina', *New Statesman and Society*, 10 November 1995.

99. Borogovac, *Rat u Bosni i Hercegovini*, p. 54.

100. Atif Dudaković, 'Ozbiljno se pripremam za slijedeći rat', interview in *Ljiljan*, no. 175, 22 May 1996, p. 10.

101. Hodžić, *Bosanski ratnici*, p. 261.

102. Izetbegović, *Sjećanja*, p. 255.

103. Ibid., pp. 254–257; Hodžić, *Bosanski ratnici*, pp. 260–261, 276–277.

104. 'President says war is over for good', *BBC Radio*, 8 April 1996, from *TV Bosnia-Herzegovina* via satellite, 6 April 1996.

105. Izetbegović, *Sjećanja*, p. 255.

106. Medina Delalić, 'Lupi petama i kazi: sve za Hrvatsku !', *Slobodna Bosna*, no. 41, 23 March 1997, pp. 22–23.

107. Hodžić, *Bosanski ratnici*, p. 261.

108. Rasim Delić, 'SFOR nije dozvolio da napravimo paradu ulicama Sarajeva i pokažemo narodu savremeno naoružanje kojim raspolažemo', interview in *Ljiljan*, no. 222, 16 April 1997, p. 9.

109. Alen Gagula, 'Bitka za grad', *Prva Linija*, No. 34, November 1995, p. 10.

110. *Vreme*, 25 September 1995.

111. Filip Švarm, 'Bosanski rat i mir: plinsko primirje', *Vreme*, 16 October 1995.

Conclusion

1. The General Framework Agreement for Peace in Bosnia-Herzegovina, Office of the High Representative, Sarajevo, 14 December 1995.

Appendix

1. Alija Izetbegović, 'Bosnian Muslims see US as an ally', interview in *Time*, 21 May 2003.

2. International Criminal Tribunal for the former Yugoslavia, indictment of Enver Hadžihasanović, Mehmed Alagić and Amir Kubura, 5 July 2001.

3. 'Bin Laden and the Balkans: The politics of anti-terrorism', International Crisis Group Report no. 119, 9 November 2001;

Gabriel Partos, 'Analysis: Bin Laden and the Balkans', *BBC News*, 2 October 2001; 'Bosnia arrests three suspected Bin Laden associates', *Agence France Presse*, 26 July 2001.

4. Srdja Trifković, 'Osama bin Laden: The Balkan connection', *Chronicles Magazine*, 19 September 2001.

5. Jean-Philippe Lavigne, 'Joint patrol in Bočinja Donja', *SFOR Informer*, no. 119, 8 August 2001.

6. Terry Boyd and Ivana Avramović, 'Fundamentalist mujahedeen attract speculation, fear in Bosnia', *Stars and Stripes*, 14 April 2002.

7. Wolfgang Petritsch, 'Islam is part of the West, too', *The New York Times*, 20 November 2001.

8. Craig Pyes, Josh Meyer and William C. Rempel, 'Terrorists use Bosnia as base and sanctuary', *The Los Angeles Times*, 7 October 2001.

9. Senad Pećanin, 'I Osama bin Laden ima bosanski pasoš !', *Dani*, 24 September 1999.

10. Izetbegović, 'Bosnian Muslims see US as an ally', op. cit.

11. 'NATO forces seize terrorist training camp in Bosnia', *Associated Press*, 17 February 1996.

12. Ena Latin, 'Sarajevo trial may lift lid on assassinations', *Balkan Crisis Report*, no. 338, 25 May 2002.

13. 'Bin Laden's contribution to the Islamisation of Bosnia', *Politika*, 6 October 2001.

14. Justin Raimondo, 'Osama in the Balkans: Our old ally is now our enemy', Antiwar.com website, 29 October 2001, www.antiwar.com/justin/j102901.html; Justin Raimondo, 'Et tu Israel? Did the Israelis have advance notice of 9/11? Probably', Antiwar.com website, 14 December 2001, http://www.antiwar.com/justin/j121401.html.

Bibliography

Bosnian Army and Other Official Publications

Archive of the Military-Historical Institute, Belgrade; NDH Collection, box 156, facsimile 6, document 38.

Armija Bosne i Hercegovine 1992–1995, NIPP 'Ljiljan', Sarajevo, 1997.

Rasim Delić, *Army – Key to the Peace*, Press Centre of the Army of the Republic of Bosnia and Herzegovina, August 1994.

Rasim Delić, *Bosnia is Here*, Press Centre of the Army of the Republic of Bosnia and Herzegovina, Sarajevo, October 1995.

Duhovna snaga odbrane, Press Centre of the Army of the Republic of Bosnia-Herzegovina, Sarajevo, February 1994.

Ethnic Cleansing of Croats in Bosnia and Herzegovina 1991–1993, Office of the President of the Croatian Community of Herzeg-Bosna, Mostar, August, 1993.

Framework Agreement establishing a Federation in the areas of the Republic of Bosnia and Herzegovina with a majority Bosniak and Croat population, and Outline of a Preliminary Agreement for a Confederation between the Republic of Croatia and the Federation, 2 March 1994.

Munir Gavrankapetanović, *Poruka borcu – ranjenom oboljelom amputircu*, Uprava za politička pitanja Armije RBiH, Sarajevo, July 1996.

The General Framework Agreement for Peace in Bosnia-Herzegovina, Office of the High Representative, Sarajevo, 14 December 1995.

Rasim Hodžić and Šefik Sabljica (eds), *Zbirka propisa iz odbrane*, Studenska Štamparija Univerzitet Sarajevo, 1995.

International Criminal Tribunal for the former Yugoslavia – indictments of Zejnil Delalić, Zdravko Mučić, Hazim Delić and Esad Landžo, 19

March 1996; of Enver Hadžihasanović, Mehmed Alagić and Amir Kubura, 5 July 2001; and of Naser Orić, 28 March 2003.

Milan Inđić, *Teritorijalna odbrana Socijalističke Republike Bosne i Hercegovine*, Republički stab Teritorijalna Odbrana Socijalistička Republika Bosna i Hercegovina, Sarajevo, 1989.

Moralni aspekti odbrane, Press Centre of the Army of the Republic of Bosnia-Herzegovina, Sarajevo, January 1995.

Vladislav Pogarčić, *Why was the Croatian Community of Herzeg-Bosnia created ?*, Republic of Bosnia-Herzegovina – Croatian Community of Herzeg-Bosnia, Office of the President, 26 July 1993.

Pravila oružanih snaga, Glavni štab oružanih snaga Republike Bosne i Hercegovine, Sarajevo, 1992.

Priručnik za komandira odjeljenja (prvo izdanje), Štab vrhovne komande oružanih snaga RBiH Uprava za obuku, školstvo, pravila i propise, Travnik, 1994.

Službeni glasnik srpskog naroda u Bosni i Hercegovini.

Strategija opštenarodne odbrane i društvene samozaštite SFRJ, Savezni sekretarijat za narodnu odbranu, Belgrade, 1987.

Memoirs, Diaries and Other Texts by Participants

Munir Alibabić-Munja, *Bosna u Kandžama KOS-a*, Behar, Sarajevo, 1996.

Janko Bobetko, *Sve moje bitke*, Vlastita naklada, Zagreb, 1996.

Muhamed Borogovac, *Rat u Bosni i Hercegovini: Politički aspekti*, Zadarska tiskara, Zadar, 2000.

Ljiljana Bulatović, *General Mladić* (2nd ed.), IP 'Nova Evropa', Belgrade, 1996.

Hasim Efendić, *Ko je branio Bosnu*, OKO, Sarajevo, 1998.

Maid Hadžiomeragić, *Stranka Demokratske Akcije i stvarnost*, Unikopis, Sarajevo, 1991.

Sefer Halilović, *Lukava Strategija*, Maršal d.o.o. PJ 'Matica Sandžaka', Sarajevo, 1997.

Alija Izetbegović, *Govori, pisma, intervjui '95*, TKP 'Šahinpašić', Sarajevo, 1996.

Alija Izetbegović, *Islam između istoka i zapada*, Svjetlost, Sarajevo, 1996.

Alija Izetbegović, *Islamska Deklaracija*, 'Bosna', Sarajevo, 1990.

Alija Izetbegović, *Sjećanja: Autobiografski zapis*, TKD Šahinpašić, Sarajevo, 2001.

Borisav Jović, *Poslednji dani SFRJ*, Politika, Belgrade, 1996.

Veljko Kadijević, *Moje viđenje raspada*, Politika, Belgrade, 1993.

Murat Kahrović, *Seferovo ratno doba*, OKO, Sarajevo, 2002.

Nedžad Latić and Zehrudin Isaković, *Ratna sjećanja Mehmeda Alagića: Rat u Srednjoj Bosni*, Bemust, Zenica, 1997.

Kerim Lučarević-Doktor, *Bitka za Sarajevo: Osuđeni na pobjedu*, TZU, Sarajevo, 2000.

Branko Mamula, *Slučaj Jugoslavija*, CID, Podgorica, 2000.

Fikret Muslimović, *Balkan u vrtlogu politike*, VKBI, Sarajevo, 2001.

Fikret Muslimović, *Agresija: Uzroci i posljedice*, Štab VK Armije BiH – Uprava za morale, Sarajevo, 1994.

Fikret Muslimović, *Kako su nas lagali*, Ljiljan, Sarajevo, 1993.

Fikret Muslimović, *Odbrana Republike*, NIPP Ljiljan, Sarajevo, 1995.

Fikret Muslimović, *Rat i politika*, Bosančica-print, Sarajevo, 2000.

Naser Orić, *Srebrenica: Svjedoči i optužuje: Genocid nad Bošnjacima u istočnoj Bosni (srednje Podrinje), April 1992. – septembar 1994.*, Općina Srebrenica, Ljubljana, 1995.

Mirko Pejanović, *Bosansko pitanje i Srbi u Bosni i Hercegovini*, Bosanska knjiga, Sarajevo, 1999.

Milisav Sekulić, *Knin je pao u Beogradu*, 2nd ed., Nidda Verlag, Bad Vilbel, 2001.

Stjepan Šiber, *Prevare, zablude, istina: ratni dnevnik 1992*, Rabić, Sarajevo, 2000.

Martin Špegelj, *Sjećanja vojnika*, Znanje, Zagreb, 2001.

Martin Špegelj, 'The War in ex-Yugoslavia and its Resolution', Zagreb, 1995 (English translation of unpublished text).

Adil Zulfikarpašić, *The Bosniak*, Hurst and Co., London, 1998.

Adil Zulfikarpašić, *Članci i intervjui povodom 70 – godišnjice*, Bošnjački institut, Sarajevo, 1991.

Newspapers, News Agencies and Radio Stations
Agence France Presse
AIM (Sarajevo)
Antiwar.com website
Associated Press
Balkan Crisis Report (London)
BiH Eksklusiv (Split)
BBC News
BBC World Service
Borba (Belgrade)
Bosnia Report (London)
Chronicles (Rockford)
Croatian Radio
Croatian TV satellite service
The Daily Telegraph
Dani (Sarajevo)
East European Reporter (London)
Feral Tribune (Split)

Front slobode (Tuzla)
Globus (Zagreb)
The Guardian
Hrvatski vojnik (Zagreb)
Ljiljan (Sarajevo)
The Los Angeles Times
The New York Times
Oslobođenje (Sarajevo)
Nacional (Zagreb)
New Statesman and Society
NIN (Belgrade)
Panorama (Zagreb)
Politika (Belgrade)
Prva linija (Sarajevo)
Radio Bosnia-Herzegovina
Reporter (Banja Luka)
Reuters
SFOR Informer (Sarajevo)
Slobodna Bosna (Sarajevo)
Slobodna Dalmacija (Split)
The South Slav Journal (London)
Stars and Stripes (Washington DC)
Time magazine
The Times (London)
TV Bosnia-Herzegovina
Vreme (Belgrade)
Wall Street Journal
War Report (London)
Yugoslav News Agency – Tanjug

Books and Academic Articles
Suad Arnautović, *Kako se branila Bosna: Vojno-politički eseji i komentari*, Promokult, Sarajevo, 1997.
'Bin Laden and the Balkans: The politics of anti-terrorism', International Crisis Group Report no. 119, 9 November 2001.
Lee Bryant, *The Betrayal of Bosnia*, University of Westminster Press, London, 1993.
Smail Čekić, *Agresija na Bosnu i genocid nad Bošnjacima 1991–1993*, NIPP Ljiljan, Sarajevo, 1994.
Norman Cigar, *Genocide in Bosnia: The politics of ethnic cleansing*, Texas A&M University Press, College Station, 1995.

Norman Cigar, *The Right to Defence: Thoughts on the Bosnian Arms Embargo*, Institute for European Defence and Strategic Studies, London, 1995.

Admiral Davor Domazet-Lošo, 'How aggression against Croatia and Bosnia-Herzegovina was prepared or the transformation of the JNA into a Serbian imperial force', *National Security and the Future*, vol. 1, no. 1, 2000.

Marina Glamočak, *La transition guerrière yougoslave*, L'Harmattan, Paris, 2002.

James Gow, *Legitimacy and the Military: The Yugoslav Crisis*, 1992.

James Gow, *The Serbian project and its adversaries: A strategy of war crimes*, C. Hurst, London, 2003.

Miroslav Hadžić, *Subdina partijske vojske*, Samizdat B92, Belgrade, 2001,

Miroslav Hadžić, *The Yugoslav People's Agony: The role of the Yugoslav People's Army*, Ashgate, Aldershot, 2002.

Attila Hoare, 'The Croatian Project to Partition Bosnia-Herzegovina', *East European Quarterly*, XXXI, no. 1, March 1997.

Attila Hoare, 'The People's Liberation Movement in Bosnia and Hercegovina, 1941–45: What Did It Mean to Fight for a Multi-National State ?', *Nationalism and Ethnic Politics*, Vol. 2, No. 3, autumn 1996.

Attila Hoare, 'A rope supports a man who is hanged: NATO air-strikes and the end of Bosnian resistance', *East European Politics and Societies*, vol. 12, no. 2, spring 1998.

Šefko Hodžić, *Bosanski ratnici*, DES, Sarajevo, 1998.

Šefko Hodžić, *Vitezovi i huni*, Sarajevo, OKO, 1996.

Omer Ibrahimagić, *Bosna i Bošnjaci između agresija i mira*, El-Kalem, Sarajevo, 1998.

Enver Imamović, *Historija Bosanske Vojske*, Art 7, Sarajevo, 1999.

Muharem Kržić, *Zločini nad banjalučkom krajinom '92–'94*, Muharem Kržić, Sarajevo, n.d..

Tarik Kulenović, 'Priprema za rat i početak rata u Bosni i Hercegovini 1992. godine', *Polemos*, vol. 1, no. 1, January-June 1998.

Marko Lopušina, *Ubij bližnjeg svog: Jugoslovenska tajna policija 1945/1995*, NIPTV Novosti DD, Belgrade, 1996.

Ivo Lučić, 'Bosnia-Herzegovina and terrorism', *National Security and the Future*, vol. 1, no. 3–4, 2001.

Ivo Lučić, 'Security and intelligence services in Bosnia-Herzegovina', *National Security and the Future*, vol. 1, no. 2, 2000.

Branka Magaš and Ivo Žanić, *The war in Croatia and Bosnia-Herzegovina 1991–1995*, Frank Cass, London, 2001.

Rusmir Mahmutćehajić, *Čitanje historije i povjerenje u Bosni: Kriva politika*, Radio Kameleon Tuzla, Tuzla, 1998.

Noel Malcolm, *Bosnia: A Short history*, MacMillan, London, 1994.

Davor Marijan, 'Borbe za Kupres u travnju 1992.', *Polemos*, vol. 3, no. 1(5), January-June 2000.

Davor Marijan, 'The war in Bosnia-Herzegovina or the unacceptable lightness of "Historicism"', *National Security and the Future*, vol. 1, no. 1, 2000.

Mark Mazower, *The War in Bosnia: An Analysis*, Action for Bosnia, London, 1992.

Takis Michas, *Unholy Alliance: Greece and Milošević's Serbia*, Texas A&M University Press, College Station, 2002.

The Military Balance 1994–1995, International Institute for Strategic Studies, London, 1994.

Milovan Milutinović, *Vojska Republike Srpske između politike i rata*, Belgrade, 1997.

Momčilo Mitrović, *Muslimanski logor Visoko, 1992–1993 (Dnevnik i kazivanja logoraša)*, 2nd ed., Vojska, Belgrade, 1995.

Vinko Pandurević, *Osnovi doktrine odbrane Republike Srpske*, Institut za geopolitičke studije, Belgrade, 1999.

Dževad Pašić, *Zemlja između istoka i zapada: Tuzla – odbrana kontinuiteta državnosti Bosne i Hercegovine*, Bosnia ARS, Tuzla, 1996.

David Rohde, *A Safe Area – Srebrenica: Europe's Worst Massacre Since the Second World War*, Pocket Books, London, 1997.

Karlo Rotim, *Obrana Herceg-Bosne*, vols. 1–2, Široki Brijeg, 1997–98.

Sarajevski proces – Suđenje muslimanskim intelektualcima 1983 g.: Sabrani dokumenti, Bosanski institut, Zürich, 1987.

Laura Silber and Allan Little, *The Death of Yugoslavia*, Penguin, London, 1995.

Mirsad Sinanović, *Smrti i pobjede*, Proton, Sarajevo, 1997.

Slobodan Srdanović, *Pale – Ratna hronika*, Svet Knjige, Belgrade, 1998.

Sead Trhulj, *Mladi Muslimani*, Sarajevo, BBR, 1995.

Snežana Trifunovska (ed.), *Yugoslavia through documents from its creation to its dissolution*, Martinus Nijhoff Publishers, Dordrecht, Boston and London, 1994.

Paul Williams and Norman Cigar, *Indictment at the Hague: The Milošević regime and the crimes of the Balkan wars*, New York University Press, New York, 2002.

Paul Williams and Norman Cigar, *A Prima Facie Case for the Indictment of Slobodan Milosević*, Alliance to Defend Bosnia-Herzegovina, London, 1996.

Đuro Zagorac, *Momčilo Perišić: Bitka ljutog generala*, Archive Media, Belgrade, 1999.

Index

2006 → with Ben.

① St. Petersburg ⎫
                  ⎬ MAYBE
② Riga   ⎭

③ Budapest
④ Dubrounik
⑤ Prague
⑥ ENGLAND (NOT LONDON)

→ OR   OR → Vienna (?)

① Prague
② Budapest (+ Venice ?)
③ Dubrounik
        ↓
ENGLAND [Chipping Sodbury]